# The Aries Book : Everything You Should Know About Ariens

CRAFTED BY SKRIUWER

**Copyright © 2025 by Skriuwer.**

All rights reserved. No part of this book may be used or reproduced in any form whatsoever without written permission except in the case of brief quotations in critical articles or reviews.

At **Skriuwer**, we're more than just a team—we're a global community of people who love books. In Frisian, "Skriuwer" means "writer," and that's at the heart of what we do: creating and sharing books with readers worldwide. Wherever you are in the world, **Skriuwer** is here to inspire learning.

**Frisian** is one of the oldest languages in Europe, closely related to English and Dutch, and is spoken by about **500,000 people** in the province of **Friesland** (Fryslân), located in the northern Netherlands. It's the second official language of the Netherlands, but like many minority languages, Frisian faces the challenge of survival in a modern, globalized world.

We're using the money we earn to promote the Frisian language.

For more information, contact : **kontakt@skriuwer.com** (www.skriuwer.com)

# TABLE OF CONTENTS

## CHAPTER 1: BASIC FACTS ABOUT ARIES

- Dates linked to Aries and the ram symbol
- Fire element and Mars influence
- Traits of energy and eagerness

## CHAPTER 2: MYTHS & LEGENDS AROUND ARIES

- The Greek tale of the golden ram
- Babylonian and Egyptian links to the ram
- Themes of bravery and rescue

## CHAPTER 3: ARIES TRAITS: STRENGTHS & WEAKNESSES

- High energy and quick starts
- Potential impatience or short temper
- Honesty and bold speech

## CHAPTER 4: HOW ARIES RELATES TO FRIENDS & FAMILY

- Approach to friendships, including directness
- Handling disagreements at home
- Being warm-hearted yet outspoken

## CHAPTER 5: ARIES IN LOVE & CLOSE BONDS

- Aries' open way of expressing feelings
- Need for independence in relationships
- Managing conflicts with a direct style

## CHAPTER 6: ARIES THROUGH HISTORY

- *Origins of Aries in ancient star lore*
- *Aries in Greek, Roman, and older cultures*
- *Modern astrology's take on Aries*

## CHAPTER 7: ARIES & CONFIDENCE

- *Building self-assurance in daily life*
- *Overcoming self-doubt and using energy well*
- *Balancing boldness with humility*

## CHAPTER 8: ARIES IN DAILY LIFE

- *Morning routines and active habits*
- *Work or school focus and time management*
- *Need for short breaks and variety*

## CHAPTER 9: GROWING UP AS AN ARIES

- *Early signs in childhood*
- *Teen years and handling strong drives*
- *Adulthood lessons and guiding the Aries spark*

## CHAPTER 10: FAMOUS ARIES & THEIR LIVES

- *Notable figures from different fields*
- *Shared Aries traits in success stories*
- *What we can learn from them*

## CHAPTER 11: HANDLING EMOTIONS AS AN ARIES

- *Quick anger and ways to calm down*
- *Showing feelings honestly*
- *Staying balanced in highs and lows*

---

## CHAPTER 12: ARIES & WORK LIFE

- *Bold approaches to tasks and leadership*
- *Challenges with patience and teamwork*
- *Thriving in roles with quick feedback*

---

## CHAPTER 13: ARIES IN DIFFERENT CULTURES

- *How the ram image appears worldwide*
- *Comparisons with Vedic and Chinese systems*
- *Modern global views on Aries*

---

## CHAPTER 14: ARIES & LEISURE ACTIVITIES

- *Sports, outdoor fun, and group outings*
- *Creative hobbies for Aries energy*
- *Relaxation tips to avoid restlessness*

---

## CHAPTER 15: ARIES & PERSONAL GOALS

- *Setting aims with bold starts*
- *Avoiding burnout and staying motivated*
- *Combining short targets with big plans*

## CHAPTER 16: OVERCOMING ARIES CHALLENGES

- *Impatience, temper, and overconfidence*
- *Tools for calmer communication*
- *Learning from mistakes to grow stronger*

## CHAPTER 17: MONEY MATTERS FOR ARIES

- *Impulse spending vs. planning*
- *Earning styles, risk-taking, and saving*
- *Practical budgeting and avoiding debt*

## CHAPTER 18: ARIES & THEIR PUBLIC IMAGE

- *First impressions and direct talk*
- *Managing online presence and leadership roles*
- *Resolving conflicts in public view*

## CHAPTER 19: ARIES ACROSS DIFFERENT STAGES OF LIFE

- *Childhood curiosity and teen independence*
- *Mid-life leadership and responsibility*
- *Senior years and passing on wisdom*

## CHAPTER 20: SUMMING IT ALL UP

- *Key Aries traits from start to finish*
- *Lessons on balancing fire and thought*
- *Using Aries' spark to build a rich life*

# CHAPTER 1: BASIC FACTS ABOUT ARIES

Aries is known as the first sign in the zodiac. When people talk about the zodiac, they are talking about a special circle of twelve signs in the sky. Each sign has certain dates linked to it, and Aries takes place from around March 21 to April 19 each year. If someone is born during these dates, many people say that person is an Aries.

Aries is often linked to the symbol of a ram. A ram is a male sheep with strong horns. This is why the sign is sometimes shown with curved horns or a picture of a ram's head. The idea is that the ram stands for energy, boldness, and eagerness, which are traits that people often connect with Aries. Just like a ram can charge forward without fear, some say Aries folks can also push ahead in life with excitement.

Aries is linked to an element that people call "fire." In astrology, fire signs are seen as active, bright, and full of life. Fire can be warm and comforting, but it can also burn if it is out of control. That is how many describe Aries and other fire signs: they can be cheerful and fun, but they can also become frustrated if something blocks their plans. Of course, not all Aries people act the same way, but these are broad ideas linked to this sign.

Mars is said to be the planet that rules Aries. In astrology, each zodiac sign has a planet that shapes the kind of energy that sign shows. Mars is named after the Roman god of war, and it stands for strength, courage, and action. People often believe that when Aries folks want something, they might go after it with lots of energy. This can be a helpful trait because it means Aries folks might not sit around waiting for things to happen. Instead, they might try to make things happen on their own.

Aries is sometimes called the "baby" of the zodiac. This does not mean Aries people are childish, but it means they are the first sign and can have a fresh way of looking at things. They might show a sense of wonder or excitement, much like a child seeing something new. Aries folks might want to start tasks right away because they like the thrill of new ideas. But, like small children, sometimes Aries people can lose interest once the first excitement is gone. That does not always happen, but it is a trait some link to Aries.

People say that color red is often linked to Aries. Red can stand for energy, passion, and action—feelings that many connect with this sign. Some people like to wear red or keep red objects nearby if they feel it helps them stay bold and ready for action. Of course, this is just an idea, and not all Aries folks like red.

When we talk about Aries, we must remember that no two Aries folks are the same. A person's birthday can affect only part of how they behave. Environment, family, and friends are also big factors. Still, the idea of Aries is that it is the spark of the zodiac, the sign that starts the wheel of the year with an energetic push. In some traditions, Aries marks the start of spring in the northern half of the world. This time is when flowers bloom, the snow melts, and animals come out of their winter rest. The change from winter to spring can feel bold, just like Aries.

People often think of Aries as brave. Sometimes, Aries folks might stand up for themselves or for people they care about. They might not like waiting around if they see a problem that needs fixing. They may rush forward to help or find a solution. But this can have two sides: it can be good to fix problems quickly, but it can also lead to hasty choices if they are not careful.

Another idea linked to Aries is independence. Many Aries people want to do things on their own, without always asking for help. They like to test themselves. This can be great for learning new skills or trying new activities. However, it can also cause them to avoid advice from others, even if that advice might help them. But that does not mean all Aries folks act like that. It is just a common idea.

Aries folks might get bored easily if something is too slow or too quiet. They may like games with action or books with exciting themes. They could also be drawn to sports or other physical activities because those things let them use their energy. Since Aries is a fire sign, many people link it with activity, movement, and strong feelings.

Let's talk about the Aries symbol a little more. The ram stands for boldness. In nature, rams can butt heads with each other. This can look like a clash of strength. Aries, as a sign, is often connected to this kind of direct energy. It is like Aries does not fear a challenge. Of course, in everyday life, Aries folks do not actually butt heads with others (at least not usually), but some might clash with people in words or opinions. This might happen if they feel strongly about something and do not want to back down.

Sometimes, people see Aries as full of excitement in the early part of a plan. Imagine someone who has a bright idea. They might start right away, telling everyone how great it is and how it will work. They might gather tools, make lists, and do tasks to get started. But when the tasks get more difficult or take longer, some Aries folks might feel restless. They might want to move on to the next idea. But if Aries people learn to stay focused, their natural energy can help them reach all sorts of goals.

Some people say that Aries folks can be honest to the point of being blunt. This means they might say what they think without holding back. Honesty can be good, but sometimes it can upset others if the truth is stated too sharply. Learning to share ideas kindly and calmly is something an Aries person might have to practice. Of course, this can be true for anyone, no matter their sign. But in many stories and descriptions about Aries, direct speech is a common trait.

The idea of Aries being the first sign also shows up in many stories. For example, some say Aries marks the start of a cycle in the zodiac. Because of this, it might represent new life, new starts, and fresh viewpoints. This is why spring is often linked to Aries. When spring arrives, plants and animals come out, the days become warmer, and life can feel renewed. That sense of a new season might match the energy of Aries well.

Aries is not just about the person born under the sign; it can also affect the mood of this period for everyone. In some beliefs, when the sun is in Aries (around March 21 to April 19), people might feel more awake or ready to try new things. This might be part of why some folks do spring cleaning or jump into new activities at this time of year.

While Aries is often described as a sign full of excitement, it also has a soft side. Many Aries people can be caring and kind, but they might not always show it in a gentle way. Instead, they might show care by taking action, like protecting a friend or standing up for someone. They might not be the type to sit quietly and comfort someone with words. Instead, they could say, "Let's fix this problem right now," or "Let's go do something fun to help you feel better."

In many parts of the world, people see Aries in the night sky as a group of stars (called a constellation). If you ever look up at the stars, you might find a pattern that looks like a crooked line or set of faint stars. Ancient people named this group of stars "Aries" because it reminded them of a ram. While not everyone can see the ram shape clearly, that is the story that was passed down through the ages.

Knowing these basic facts about Aries can give you an idea of what this sign stands for: boldness, excitement, eagerness, independence, and a fiery spirit. People connect it to the ram, the color red, the planet Mars, and the idea of springtime in the north. These are all general ideas, so any real Aries person might act differently. Real life is more complicated than any zodiac summary. Still, many like learning about these traits to understand themselves or people they know.

You might see Aries described as a leader among the zodiac signs. This is because Aries can be good at taking the first step when others are not sure. Being willing to go first is a strong trait, and it can help others feel brave enough to follow. Aries might like to test new ideas rather than wait for someone else to try them. If the idea works, great. If it does not, they can move on and try something else.

Some people might ask, "What if I was born on the day when Aries changes to the next sign?" This is sometimes called being "on the cusp." The dates for each zodiac sign can shift slightly from year to year. If someone is born around April 19 or April 20, they might wonder if they are Aries or the next sign, which is Taurus. The truth is, you can find out by looking at a chart that shows the exact moment the sun moved into Taurus that year. But many people do not worry about it too much. If they feel like they have Aries traits, they might think of themselves as Aries, and if they feel more like Taurus, that is fine too.

Aries is also said to have a busy mind, always thinking of what to do next. This can be exciting, but it can make it hard to relax at times. An Aries person might lie awake at night thinking of all the things they want to do the next day. They might also talk a lot about their ideas to anyone who will listen. This can be fun, but learning to pause and rest can also help them stay healthy.

Aries folks might enjoy friendly challenges. They could like board games, sports, or any activity where there is a bit of fun competition. They tend to put their heart into what they do. Even if they lose, they might be quick to ask for a rematch. They like the thrill of trying again and pushing themselves further.

Though Aries is known for being direct, that does not always mean loud or bossy. Some Aries people are quieter. They might show their energy in smaller ways, like focusing deeply on a project. But the Aries spark can still be there, making them eager to begin new tasks or make bold moves when needed.

One more point is that Aries is often said to be straightforward in feelings. Some Aries folks say they do not like playing games with emotions. If they like someone, they might say so. If they do not like something, they might also speak up. This can sometimes cause friction if others are not ready for such honesty. But it can also be refreshing because everyone knows where they stand with an Aries.

These are some basic ideas that give an overall picture of Aries. We have covered the date range, symbols, elements, and common traits. We have also noted that every Aries is unique and may show these traits in different ways. But if you meet someone with that ram-like drive, full of excitement and a "let's go!" attitude, there is a good chance they have strong Aries energy in their birth chart.

# CHAPTER 2: MYTHS & LEGENDS AROUND ARIES

Aries is linked to many stories from long ago. People have looked at the stars for thousands of years and made up tales about the patterns they saw. The group of stars we call Aries is one of these patterns, and ancient folks told stories to explain why this shape in the sky was called the ram.

One of the most famous stories about Aries comes from Greek mythology. It tells of a golden ram that saved two children, Phrixus and Helle. Their story goes like this:

Long ago, there was a king with two children. The children's mother was kind, but the king remarried, and their new stepmother did not like the children. She wanted them gone. To protect the children, a magical ram with golden wool came from the sky. This ram told the children to hold on to its back, and it flew away to carry them to safety. As they traveled, Helle lost her grip and fell into the sea, and that place was later called the Hellespont. Phrixus made it safely to a land called Colchis. In thanks for this rescue, he offered the ram to the gods, and the ram's golden fleece became a treasure in Colchis.

In this story, the ram's act of saving the children is seen as a great act of bravery and kindness. Later, a famous group of Greek heroes went on a mission to find the Golden Fleece. That story involves Jason and the Argonauts, who faced many dangers to reach Colchis and get the fleece. The ram that became the constellation Aries is said to be the same one that saved Phrixus and Helle. As a reward for its heroic deed, the gods placed the ram's image among the stars.

Because of this tale, some say Aries stands for bravery and rescue. The ram in the story risked everything to help the children. That links to Aries being a sign of bold action and a spirit that wants to help or protect. Even though Aries can sometimes be seen as headstrong, the story reminds us that this sign also has a caring side.

In other stories, Aries is also linked to spring. In ancient times, people looked at the sky to tell the seasons. Around a certain time of year, when the sun rose in front of the constellation Aries, spring would begin in the northern half of the world. People noticed that the weather got warmer, plants started to grow again, and animals came out of their dens. They linked this change with the sign of Aries. Since spring can bring bright energy and fresh growth, many people thought Aries was a sign that brought life and action.

In Babylonian times (in ancient Mesopotamia), the ram was also seen in the stars. Some suggest that long before Greek stories were told, the Babylonians had named this group of stars as something related to a farm animal. Over time, different groups of people changed or added to these stories. But the idea of the ram stuck because this pattern of stars made people think of horns, or at least of a shape that could be linked to a ram.

The star that is brightest in the Aries constellation is called Hamal. The name Hamal comes from an Arabic word that means "lamb." Another star in the group is named Sheratan, which comes from a word meaning "two signs," likely referring to how it works with another star to mark the early spring equinox in old times. This equinox is around March 20 or 21 each year, close to when the sun moves into the sign of Aries. Folks in old times paid close attention to the sky because that helped them know when to plant crops or do other important tasks.

In Roman mythology, the ram can appear in stories about Mars or Mercury. Mars was the god of war, linked to the planet that rules

Aries. Mercury was the messenger god, linked to quick thinking and travel. Even though the ram is not always the main animal in Roman tales, the spirit of Aries—bold, eager, and energetic—fits well with the qualities of Mars.

Throughout history, people have often linked Aries to ideas like leadership, new starts, and bright spirit. Some say that the ram in the stars was seen as leading the other signs around the zodiac wheel. Because Aries is the first sign (in many traditions), it has that sense of being at the front of the line, calling out, "It's time to begin!" That is why, in many old texts, Aries is called the "head" of the zodiac.

In some Egyptian stories, there were gods shown with ram heads. For example, the god Khnum was shown as a man with the head of a ram. He was linked to the source of the Nile River and the idea of creation of life. Though this is not the same as the Greek myth of the golden ram, it still shows that rams were important symbols. The ram was seen as a symbol of strength, life, and the power to spark changes in nature.

Beyond Greek and Egyptian ideas, other cultures had their own tales. In the old Persian empire, the new year was often marked in early spring. Though they might not have used the name "Aries," the return of spring was a time of excitement for many people. The idea of a ram or sheep might have been part of rituals or stories to mark the time when fields turned green again.

When we look at these myths, we can see a common theme: Aries is often linked with a strong, brave ram. This ram is not just a random animal. It stands for an energy that protects, acts, and sparks new life. Whether it is saving children, guiding the zodiac, or honoring the start of a new season, the ram shows the spirit we often link to Aries.

Some children like to hear about the Greek myth of the golden ram because it sounds magical. A flying ram with golden wool is a striking image. The fact that it saved children from danger gives the story a brave and caring theme. Then, when the ram's fleece was kept as a great treasure, it became something heroes wanted to find. This tale helped shape how people saw Aries for many, many years afterward.

If we think about this story in simple terms, it might teach us that bravery and kindness can go together. The ram could have flown away to a safer place on its own, but it chose to help the children. That helped them escape a bad situation. Aries, in modern astrology, is often said to be bold and quick to act. Myths like these show that quick action can be used to help others, not just to stand out.

Another myth about Aries from Greek lore focuses on the shape of the constellation. People said the stars we see as Aries today once formed part of a larger shape. Over time, storytellers changed the story. That is common with constellations. Different groups see different shapes in the stars. What one group calls Aries might be seen differently by another group. For instance, some ancient peoples in Africa might have seen a different animal in those stars. The name changes, but the spirit of wonder does not.

There are also smaller myths that mention a ram giving warmth or light to people who are lost in the cold. While these might not be as famous as the golden ram story, they follow the same idea: the ram helps, guides, or brings hope. Since Aries is linked to spring and new life, stories often show the ram as a helpful figure.

When we read these legends, we can see why Aries is considered a sign of fresh starts. The ancient stories placed the ram at important moments: saving children, bringing the new season, or leading the zodiac. This kind of role is perfect for a sign known for stepping forward, being direct, and wanting to make changes.

In older star charts, artists drew the ram with a curled horn, placed among other zodiac creatures like the Bull (Taurus), the Twins (Gemini), and the Fishes (Pisces). Aries itself is not made up of very bright stars, so you have to look carefully on a clear night to see it. But once you know where to look, it can be fun to imagine the shape of a ram in the sky.

Astrology texts from centuries ago often talk about Aries as ruled by Mars. In some stories, the ram was said to be under the protection of Mars, who granted the ram its bold, fiery spirit. This matched the idea that Aries people are ruled by a planet linked to energy and willpower. There is also a link between the color red (Mars is often called the Red Planet) and the sign Aries. The golden ram from the myth has a shining coat, which could be linked to the bright spirit of Aries, even though the color is gold rather than red.

Myths and legends about Aries show up in art too. Painters from the Renaissance or other time periods often made works of art about Greek myths. Some painted the golden ram, Jason and the Argonauts, or the moment the ram rescues the children. By looking at these paintings, you can see how people imagined the story. The ram might be shown with shining golden wool, flying through the sky, or standing proud on a hill.

Even in modern times, the tale of the golden fleece is retold in books and movies about Greek heroes. Children and adults might read these stories and see Aries as an important part of that heroic age. The ram was not just an animal; it was a magical helper.

Outside of Greek mythology, Aries also appears in signs and symbols in many places. Some old coins from ancient civilizations showed a ram to mark the time of year or as a symbol of strength. Some flags or seals might use a ram to stand for a group's character. While these might not directly call it "Aries," the shape of the ram's horns remains a strong image.

These myths and legends can teach us that Aries is more than just a ram in the sky. It is a sign with stories of bravery, care, and a link to the arrival of spring. Even if you do not believe in astrology, the stories themselves can be fun and inspiring. They remind us that new life returns each year, that help can come from surprising places, and that it is possible to act with courage.

It is interesting to see how a single group of stars became so important to different cultures. The Greeks made it part of their heroic stories. The Babylonians had it as part of their star maps. The Egyptians had ram-headed gods that showed strength and life. Each group, in its own way, looked at Aries and saw something powerful.

People today might not rely on star stories as much as ancient folks did. But we still use the zodiac for fun or for personal reflection. Myths and legends can guide us to think about what traits we want to show in our own lives. For Aries, these traits might be boldness, helpful actions, and the spark of new projects. Myths can encourage us to act when action is needed, or to give a hand to those in trouble.

If you ever get the chance to look at the night sky in a dark place with no city lights, you can search for Aries. It is near the constellation of Taurus and below Andromeda. You might find a crooked line of stars that does not look very much like a ram at first. But with a star map or an online guide, you can spot those faint points of light that form Aries. Then, imagine that golden ram flying through the sky to help someone in need. That image can be quite exciting for a child or anyone who loves a good story.

# CHAPTER 3: ARIES TRAITS - STRENGTHS & WEAKNESSES

When people talk about Aries, they often describe a person who is sure of what they want and eager to do things right away. In this chapter, we will look at the main qualities that can make Aries stand out. These qualities might help an Aries person reach goals or handle challenges. Still, there can be sides to each trait that need careful thought. We will explore both the helpful sides and the difficult sides, so we can get a full picture of what it is like to be an Aries in everyday life.

## 1. High Energy and Action

One of the strongest qualities linked to Aries is a strong, active spirit. This can show up in many ways. For example, an Aries might jump at the chance to try a new sport or take on a big school project. Once they decide to do it, they usually throw themselves into the task with plenty of enthusiasm. This high energy can make them fun to be around. It might feel like they always have something going on, and they might encourage others to get moving too.

**Upside**:

- Aries often bring excitement to a team or a gathering. Their get-up-and-go spirit can push everyone else to join in.
- They like to tackle tasks right away, which can be useful when something needs to be done quickly.

**Downside:**

- Sometimes, Aries might not stop to think before acting. They can charge ahead without a plan, which might lead to mistakes or confusion.
- Their high energy can be too strong for people who like to move at a slower pace. An Aries might need to practice waiting or slowing down.

## 2. Bold Behavior

Aries folks are often described as bold. When they feel strongly about something, they might stand up for it even if others disagree. They might speak their mind plainly and not worry too much about what people think. This can be a good trait because they will not back down easily if they believe they are correct or if they see something unfair.

**Upside:**

- An Aries can be a brave friend who defends someone who is being picked on.
- They might try new ideas before everyone else. This can bring fresh solutions to a group.

**Downside:**

- Boldness can turn into stubbornness if they do not know when to give ground.
- Being too direct might hurt people's feelings, especially if the Aries person does not soften their words.

## 3. Cheerful Outlook

Many Aries show a bright, hopeful view of life. They see the glass as half full and expect things to go their way. This can help them stay happy even when problems arise. They often think, "I can handle this," which can be good for boosting their confidence. Other people might look to them for encouragement and positivity.

**Upside**:

- This trait can keep spirits high, even during hard times.
- Friends and family might feel a little happier when they are around someone who looks on the bright side.

**Downside**:

- If Aries always expects the best, they might be shocked when problems get worse.
- They may overlook dangers or not think of the details that could go wrong.

## 4. Quick to Start Things

Aries often enjoy being the first to act. They might be the ones who say, "Let's do this!" and then begin right away. This trait can help them seize chances that others hesitate to take. For example, if a fun event is coming up, the Aries person might sign up first while everyone else is still thinking. Their quickness can open new doors.

**Upside**:

- They do not waste time. When they see a path forward, they go for it.
- They often turn plans into real action.

**Downside**:

- They can leave others behind if they rush too quickly.
- Sometimes, Aries might start many projects and find it hard to finish them all.

## 5. Self-Reliance

Aries are known for being self-reliant. They often think, "I can handle this alone." This trait can make them good at solving problems on their own. An Aries might teach themselves new skills or figure out how to fix a problem in a creative way. They do not always wait for help. They prefer to handle matters in their own style.

**Upside**:

- They can manage many tasks without leaning on others.
- Self-reliance can help them build strong life skills, such as learning to fix or organize things.

**Downside**:

- They might refuse help even when it is needed, which can lead to stress or mistakes.
- Aries might give off the impression that they do not need anyone, which can make friends and family feel left out.

## 6. Friendliness

While some folks think Aries might be tough, a lot of Aries people have a friendly side. They can be lively and eager to talk to new people. They like sharing jokes and stories. When they are in a good mood, they can seem bright and welcoming, which helps them make friends fast.

**Upside**:

- They can bring people together through fun activities or chats.
- They can spread a sense of fun that others want to join in.

**Downside**:

- If an Aries is in a bad mood, their bright side might vanish quickly.
- Their straightforward style might come off as pushy to people who do not know them well.

## 7. Strong Sense of Fairness

Some Aries have a strong idea of what is fair. They might speak up if they see a friend being treated badly or if rules are not the same for everyone. They do not like seeing someone treated in an unfair way. This can make them stand out as helpers in tough situations.

**Upside**:

- They can be protectors for those who cannot stand up for themselves.
- They bring attention to problems that others might ignore.

**Downside**:

- They can get carried away in their desire to fix unfair situations, turning a small issue into a bigger conflict.
- Sometimes, they might overlook other people's viewpoints while focusing on what they think is fair.

## 8. Mood Changes

While Aries can be bright and happy, they can also have moments when they feel upset or restless. Because they feel things strongly, small issues can trigger bigger reactions. One moment, they might be laughing; the next moment, they could be annoyed. Learning to handle these mood changes can be an important life lesson for Aries.

**Upside**:

- Their changing moods can make them honest about how they feel, so nothing is hidden.
- The bright side is that their anger or sadness usually does not last too long.

**Downside**:

- Quick mood shifts can confuse friends and family, who might not know why the Aries person is upset.
- They might say things in anger that they later regret.

## 9. Short Attention Span

Because Aries enjoy excitement and action, they might lose interest in tasks that feel slow or boring. For example, they might be super excited to begin a long reading assignment but lose focus a few pages in. They might need to train themselves to stick with tasks even when the excitement wears off.

**Upside**:

- They bring fresh ideas whenever they are interested.
- Their fast thinking can lead to quick improvements or solutions.

**Downside**:

- Finishing tasks might be hard if they keep skipping to something new.
- They might miss important details if they rush.

## 10. Honest Expressions

Aries often say what is on their mind without fear. They might tell a friend, "I do not like that idea," even if that friend's feelings might be hurt. Many people find this honesty refreshing. Others might find it too strong, especially if they prefer gentle feedback. Aries may need to learn to express honesty with respect.

**Upside**:

- You can trust they will not hide what they think.
- They can help others spot problems quickly by pointing them out.

**Downside**:

- Their words can sting if not said kindly.
- Sometimes, they might share opinions when it is better to stay silent.

## 11. Eagerness to Lead

Aries can be good at stepping into leader roles. They like to decide what direction a group should take and outline tasks. They might handle pressure well and keep moving when challenges arise. Because they do not shy away from tasks, they can be the first to say, "I'll handle this." This can make them stand out in a team.

**Upside**:

- If a group is stuck, an Aries leader might give it new life and drive everyone forward.
- They might protect group members by taking responsibility.

**Downside**:

- They can be bossy if they do not learn to listen.
- They may want to direct everything, causing others to feel ignored.

## 12. Readiness for Challenges

An Aries might feel excited when facing a big challenge. Whether it is a puzzle, a sport, or a test, they often like to test their limits. This can help them gain skills and confidence. They might keep going until they figure out the solution.

**Upside**:

- They often make progress quickly because they are not afraid to try.
- Their can-do spirit can lift others' spirits during tough tasks.

**Downside**:

- They might push too hard, leading to burnout or injury if it is a physical task.
- Sometimes, they do not know when to take a break or ask for help.

## 13. Search for Fun

Aries often seek out enjoyable moments, such as games, adventures in safe places, or funny jokes with friends. They might be the first to suggest something thrilling, like trying a new ride at a fair. This zest can bring laughter and good times to others.

**Upside**:

- They help make life more interesting, pulling friends out of dull routines.
- They often have stories to share about the fun things they have done.

**Downside**:

- Focusing too much on excitement might distract them from duties like homework or chores.
- They might grow restless if they cannot find something fun to do.

## 14. Strong Boundaries

Even though Aries can be friendly, they also keep clear personal boundaries. They might not let someone push them around or tell them what to do. They can be firm in guarding their rights, ideas, and wishes. This can help them stand firm in difficult settings.

**Upside**:

- They might avoid being taken advantage of since they stick up for themselves.
- Knowing what they want helps them set limits with people who are disrespectful.

**Downside:**

- In group activities, they might struggle if they cannot have the final say.
- They may appear unwilling to compromise because they hold their ground too firmly.

## 15. Warm-Hearted Moments

Though Aries can seem tough or headstrong, they often have a warm heart deep inside. They may do nice things for people they care about. For instance, they might buy a favorite treat for a friend who is sad, or cheer up a family member who is having a bad day. Aries might not always show warmth in a gentle manner, but their actions can be thoughtful.

**Upside:**

- Loved ones can feel protected and special when an Aries decides to show care.
- Aries often want to fix problems for those they love, which can be very helpful.

**Downside:**

- They might show care by telling someone what to do, which can come across as controlling rather than kind.
- If they are busy, they might forget to show small signs of warmth, even if they do care deeply.

## 16. Willingness to Take Risks

Aries might jump into new activities or tasks without too much worry about what could go wrong. They might enjoy exploring new places, learning new hobbies, or meeting new people. This can open doors to interesting experiences.

**Upside**:

- Life can be full of unique moments because they do not wait forever to try something.
- They can discover hidden talents or make unexpected friends by taking chances.

**Downside**:

- Taking big risks can lead to trouble if Aries does not think about safety.
- Some Aries might keep chasing thrills and forget about wise planning.

## 17. Drive for Success

An Aries often works hard to reach goals. They might decide they want the top grade in class or aim for a high score in a sport. Once that target is set, they give it their best shot. This inner drive can help them stand out.

**Upside**:

- They can push through obstacles because they want to reach the goal so much.
- Their drive can inspire others to try harder too.

**Downside**:

- They might become impatient with people who do not share the same drive.
- Failing to meet their high aims can upset them more than it might upset others.

## 18. Need for Personal Space

Even though Aries can be social, they also need room to act freely. They might not like being told to sit still or follow many rules. This does not mean they always cause trouble. Rather, they need a sense of freedom in order to do their best.

**Upside**:

- They do well in settings where they can act on their own ideas without strict limits.
- They can come up with creative methods because they are not stuck in one spot.

**Downside**:

- If rules are necessary (like in school or at work), an Aries can feel annoyed.
- They might try to break free from limits in a way that causes friction with authority figures.

## 19. Competitive Nature

Aries often like to compare results and see who can do best. This might appear in games, sports, or even friendly quizzes. They like testing their skills against others. This is not always a bad thing. It can help them push themselves to reach better results.

**Upside**:

- A little healthy competition can keep life exciting.
- Aries might train harder or study more if they know they can reach a top spot.

**Downside**:

- If they take competition too seriously, they might become sore losers or brag too much when they win.
- Some friends might not enjoy this level of competition, leading to hurt feelings.

## 20. Ability to Bounce Back

When Aries face loss or disappointment, they might feel upset at first. However, they often pick themselves up and move forward quickly. They might say, "I'll try again tomorrow," rather than give up. This ability to bounce back can help them succeed in many parts of life.

**Upside**:

- They do not let mistakes or failures weigh them down for long.
- Their positive outlook can serve as a reminder that a fresh start is always possible.

**Downside**:

- Sometimes, they might not learn enough from their mistakes if they move on too fast.
- They might overlook the value in pausing to think about what went wrong.

## Putting It All Together

Aries have a broad set of traits that can be both helpful and challenging. Their strong energy can spur them into action, help them speak up, and bring excitement to a group. Yet it can also lead to tension or hasty choices if not guided carefully. Learning to balance these traits is often the key for an Aries to feel satisfied and do well in different areas of life.

For instance, someone with strong Aries traits might benefit from taking small pauses during the day to think about what they are doing. This does not mean they have to change who they are. But by adding a moment of thought, they might avoid rushing too fast or stepping on someone's toes. They can still keep their bright spark while remembering others' feelings.

In short, the qualities linked with Aries form a pattern of high energy, eagerness, and honest expression. These can be strong tools if used wisely. Every Aries is unique, of course, and family, friends, and other parts of life shape each person's personality too. Still, the traits described here give us a good idea of what often appears in people who show clear Aries qualities.

# CHAPTER 4: HOW ARIES RELATES TO FRIENDS & FAMILY

Aries people are not only strong-willed and action-focused, but they also have unique ways of connecting with loved ones. In this chapter, we will look at how Aries folks might act with close friends, parents, siblings, and other family members. We will also consider ways in which Aries can handle conflicts or show care, since strong feelings play a big role in how Aries interacts with others.

## 1. First Impressions with New Friends

Aries people often come across as bright and alert when meeting someone new. Because they have a direct style, they may say, "Hi, I'm glad to meet you," and jump into a conversation. This bold way of talking can be appealing to people who like open, friendly folks. At the same time, it might seem a bit intense for people who are more reserved.

- **Good Side**: Aries can be fun to talk to right away. Their eager smile and energy make them easy to notice in a crowd.
- **Challenge**: Some people might misread Aries' direct style as bossiness or impatience if they are used to a gentler approach.

## 2. Building Close Friendships

Once Aries forms a friendship, they can be very supportive. They often like shared activities or games. They might say, "Let's play this sport together" or "Let's make an art project." These shared tasks allow the Aries person to use their enthusiasm and spend time in a lively way.

- **Good Side**: Aries friends can bring lots of fun and new ideas. They might plan group activities or encourage everyone to try new things.
- **Challenge**: If a friend is not as quick to act, Aries might become impatient. They could say, "Why are you taking so long?" which can cause friction. Aries may need to practice patience or learn that not everyone moves at the same pace.

## 3. Sharing Feelings with Friends

Aries people can be straightforward in telling friends about their day, problems, or joys. Because they do not like hiding their thoughts, they might say what is on their mind. This can make friendships feel real and honest. But sometimes, Aries might forget that not everyone wants such open talk all the time.

- **Good Side**: Aries' honesty can create strong bonds, as their friends always know where they stand.
- **Challenge**: They might share strong opinions in a blunt way. If a friend is sensitive, this could lead to disagreements or hurt feelings.

## 4. Handling Friend Conflicts

Disagreements happen in any friendship. Aries might respond with strong words if they feel wronged. They do not usually stay silent when upset. They might say, "That's not fair," and demand a fix right away. This direct style can fix small problems quickly. But it can also cause more tension if the other friend needs quiet or gentle steps to fix things.

- **Good Side**: At least the problem is out in the open. Aries does not bottle things up.
- **Challenge**: Aries might argue too loudly or strongly, making the other person step away. They need to remember that calm words can help solve a conflict.

## 5. Supporting Friends in Need

When a friend is sad or facing problems, Aries might step in with a plan. They could say, "Let's do this to fix the problem," or "I'm here to back you up." This active approach can be wonderful because it shows that Aries is ready to help. However, some friends might need gentle listening first, instead of quick fixes.

- **Good Side**: Aries can be a firm supporter, ready to stand up for friends who feel alone.
- **Challenge**: They might push solutions too quickly. Some situations need patience or quiet empathy rather than immediate action.

## 6. Aries and Group Friendships

Aries often stand out in a group. They may be the one who speaks first or suggests the next activity. This can be great for stirring up excitement. But it can also create issues if other people want a turn leading or choosing. An Aries might need to remember to ask, "What would you like to do?" so everyone feels included.

- **Good Side**: Groups with an Aries rarely lack ideas or fun.
- **Challenge**: Aries might unintentionally overshadow quieter friends, leaving them out of the conversation.

## 7. Aries at Home with Parents

In a family setting, Aries children may show signs of independence early on. They might say, "I'll do it myself!" even if they need a bit of help. This can be a great trait because it helps them build skills. But parents might find it hard to guide an Aries child who strongly resists advice.

- **Good Side**: Aries children can learn tasks quickly because they love trying things on their own.
- **Challenge**: They can become frustrated if parents set too many rules or if they feel their independence is blocked.

## 8. Talking to Parents

Aries often speak their minds, even at home. If they do not like a rule, they might say so plainly. They could push to change it or ask questions about why it exists. This can be good because it shows the child is thinking. However, parents might wish for a calmer talk at times.

- **Good Side**: Everyone knows what Aries children think or want, so parents do not have to guess.
- **Challenge**: Big arguments might arise if the Aries child speaks in a tone that sounds rude or too strong.

## 9. Seeking Approval

Although Aries are independent, they still want to be noticed for what they do well. They might show a drawing or a sports award and say, "Look, I did this!" They enjoy hearing supportive words from parents or guardians. This can push them to do even better. But if they do not get the approval they want, Aries might lose interest or feel irritated.

- **Good Side**: If parents recognize and encourage an Aries child's work, it can boost the child's confidence.
- **Challenge**: An Aries might become too focused on praise, losing sight of the fun in the activity. Or they might feel down if they do not get the feedback they expect.

## 10. Aries with Siblings

When it comes to brothers and sisters, Aries can be warm and protective. If a sibling is younger, the Aries might watch over them during family gatherings. Aries can also be good at entertaining siblings, as they have plenty of ideas for games. However, sibling conflicts can happen if Aries tries to take the lead all the time or if they get annoyed by a sibling's slower pace.

- **Good Side**: Aries siblings can bring fun and laughter into the house.
- **Challenge**: They might fight for control, which can lead to arguments about who picks the TV show or who goes first in a game.

## 11. Discipline at Home

If parents or guardians use strict rules, Aries might push back. They do not always respond well to "Because I said so." They want reasons and a sense of fairness. A good approach might involve explaining the rule in simple terms. Aries might accept it more calmly if they see the point.

- **Good Side**: They might follow a rule if they understand it keeps them or others safe.
- **Challenge**: Yelling or harsh methods might make them more rebellious, as Aries can be headstrong.

## 12. Showing Love to Family

Aries can show care through helpful actions. For instance, they might offer to carry groceries or fix a problem around the house. They may not always be the type to give long hugs or speak softly, but their actions can speak louder. They might say, "Let me help you with that," which shows their concern.

- **Good Side**: Family members can see that Aries is willing to take charge of tasks when needed.
- **Challenge**: If family members expect many gentle words, they might feel that Aries seems distant at times. Aries might need to remember that sometimes, people want kind words too.

## 13. Aries as a Teen in the Family

As an Aries grows older, they might want even more freedom. Parents could notice that Aries teens want to stay out later, choose their own activities, or make decisions without checking in. This can be a normal part of growing up, but with Aries' strong will, it may feel more intense.

- **Good Side**: Aries teens might get ready for adult life early by learning how to stand on their own.
- **Challenge**: Conflicts can pop up if parents worry about safety or want to set boundaries. Aries teens might see these rules as limiting, leading to arguments.

## 14. Aries as a Parent or Guardian

When an Aries becomes a parent or guardian, they might bring high energy into family life. They can be playful with their children, trying to spark excitement and laughter at home. They might encourage the child to explore talents or interests without fear. At the same time, Aries parents may have to watch their own temper, since kids can test patience.

- **Good Side**: Aries parents can keep the household lively.
- **Challenge**: If they get upset, they might speak too sharply to children, who need calm guidance instead.

## 15. Big Family Events

Aries might enjoy big gatherings, like birthdays or weekend visits, because they like to be around loved ones. They might bring games or suggest group activities to keep everyone entertained. However, if the event drags on or becomes dull, Aries may get restless and look for a way to spice things up.

- **Good Side**: They bring a spark to family events. Others might be glad for their ideas.
- **Challenge**: Aries might become bored if the event does not match their style, leading to impatience or an early exit.

## 16. Handling Family Disagreements

In family disagreements, Aries might voice their side strongly. If they think someone was treated unfairly, they could step in to defend that person. But if the disagreement is about Aries' own actions, they might feel attacked and fight back with strong words. To keep the peace, they might need to slow down, listen, and see other viewpoints.

- **Good Side**: They help address problems instead of ignoring them.
- **Challenge**: They might spark bigger fights if they do not wait to calm down before talking.

## 17. Celebrations and Gift-Giving

Aries may enjoy giving gifts that have an exciting twist or that match a person's unique interests. For instance, they might pick out a bright, fun item rather than something plain. They prefer giving something memorable. On the receiving end, they like gifts that show thought and reflect their active side.

- **Good Side**: Aries often puts thought into gifts because they want others to share in their energetic spirit.
- **Challenge**: They might be disappointed if others do not react with the same enthusiasm they feel.

## 18. Blending Aries Traits with Family Traditions

Some families have strong customs or ways of doing things. Aries may go along if they feel it is meaningful. However, they can question old practices that do not seem useful or fair. This can lead to positive changes in the family, or it can cause friction if older members feel disrespected.

- **Good Side**: Aries might bring fresh ideas to traditional routines.
- **Challenge**: They may clash with family members who do not want to change long-standing habits.

## 19. Helping Younger Relatives

Aries might be a fun uncle, aunt, cousin, or older sibling to younger relatives. They can show them new games or guide them with energetic support. They often want younger relatives to be brave and try new things. However, Aries might need to remember that not all children have the same daring spirit.

- **Good Side**: Younger relatives can look up to the Aries as a strong, active role model.
- **Challenge**: If they push a child to do something before the child is ready, it might cause fear or tears.

## 20. Keeping Harmony in the Home

While Aries is known for being spirited, they also want a happy home. They can work toward harmony by using their strength in kind ways. For example, an Aries might settle an argument between siblings by fairly hearing both sides. Or they might plan a simple gathering with the family to build closer bonds.

- **Good Side**: Their direct style can fix misunderstandings before they grow.
- **Challenge**: They might need to remember that some family members want slower, gentler talks. Aries should be patient and let others speak.

## Ways Aries Can Grow Stronger Bonds

1. **Practice Listening**: Aries can make a real effort to listen fully when a loved one speaks, instead of planning their reply right away. This can help them understand others better and reduce disagreements.

2. **Share the Spotlight**: If an Aries is in a group, they can pause to let someone else share an idea or lead an activity. This shows respect for each person's voice.

3. **Use Kind Words**: Even honest opinions can be shared nicely. For example, instead of saying, "That's a bad idea," Aries could say, "I see some problems with that plan. Can we look for a

better option?"

4. **Give Space to Different Styles**: Not everyone has the same speed or energy. Sometimes, a slower approach works fine. Aries can respect that by not rushing others or scolding them.

5. **Be Patient in Conflict**: Taking a breath or counting to ten can help Aries cool down if they feel upset. Calm words often solve problems faster than shouting.

6. **Show Empathy**: A friend or family member might need a listening ear, not just a quick fix. Aries can learn to ask, "How do you feel?" instead of jumping to solutions.

7. **Praise Loved Ones**: Aries knows they enjoy hearing kind words. Their loved ones do, too. A small comment like, "I appreciate what you did," can brighten someone's day.

8. **Choose Fun Activities for Everyone**: When planning a group outing, Aries can think about all ages and preferences. They might pick something that both older folks and younger folks can enjoy.

## A Full Picture of Aries in Friendships and Family

Aries have a special style when it comes to the people they care about. They bring a strong, lively presence, which can make things more exciting or solve problems fast. At the same time, they need to handle conflicts gently and remember that others might have softer feelings or different opinions.

In friendships, Aries often play the role of the active friend who stirs up fun. They can be counted on to voice their thoughts openly. But this means they may need to work on patience and a kinder tone, especially with sensitive friends. When conflicts happen, Aries can learn to control their temper by focusing on the good parts of the friendship instead of just the problem at hand.

Within the family, Aries might push for independence from a young age. They could try to do chores or tasks on their own. They might also speak up if rules feel unfair. Parents and siblings could value the Aries child's spirit, yet they might have to guide them toward calmer ways of solving problems. When Aries grows up and has a family, they can keep the home lively and guide children with confidence. They just have to remember that little ones need patience and soft words.

Aries can also create warm ties with relatives if they use their helpfulness wisely. Whether it is organizing a family game or offering to fix a broken fence, Aries can show love through action. They simply need to avoid pushing their ideas too forcefully onto everyone else. By finding a balance between bold energy and gentle respect, an Aries can be a wonderful friend and family member.

## Conclusion

Friends and family are an important part of life for many Aries people. Because Aries has a direct and energetic style, they can bring excitement, solve problems, and stand up for loved ones. Their open nature can lead to quick bonding, but it can also cause friction if they do not take others' needs into account. By learning to slow down, listen, and show empathy, Aries can build even stronger ties. In this way, their spark will shine without burning those around them.

# CHAPTER 5: ARIES IN LOVE & CLOSE BONDS

Aries is often described as a bold and active sign, and these traits can show up strongly in close bonds. When we speak of "love," we can mean romantic attraction, but we can also include deep friendships or strong emotional connections with others. Aries people might show their feelings in direct, bright ways. In this chapter, we will look at how Aries might act when they care deeply about someone, what strengths they bring to these bonds, and what challenges might appear.

## 1. First Steps in Close Bonds

Aries often step forward and show interest without waiting. In romantic matters, an Aries individual might come right out and say, "I like you. Would you like to spend time with me?" This open style can be refreshing for those who prefer honesty. At the same time, it can feel overwhelming for someone who is used to slower, gentler steps.

- **Helpful side**: Aries removes guesswork. People rarely have to wonder if Aries is interested.
- **Challenge**: If the other person needs more time or a slower pace, Aries might seem too quick or pushy.

## 2. Passion and Excitement

Because Aries has a fiery spirit, close bonds can be filled with excitement. The Aries partner might plan lively dates, bring fun ideas for activities, or send friendly messages full of energy. They might appear at someone's door with a big smile, ready to do something active, such as going for a walk, playing a sport, or visiting a place with lots of action. This enthusiastic side can make a bond feel bright.

- **Helpful side**: There is rarely a dull moment with an Aries who is focused on the bond.
- **Challenge**: The nonstop energy can tire out a partner or friend who needs calm days. Aries might have to learn that rest is also important.

## 3. Direct Feelings

Aries often speak their mind. If they feel happy or excited, they show it. If they are upset or angry, they might show that too. In a close bond, this can mean fewer hidden thoughts. Many people value honesty, so an Aries partner can be appreciated for saying what they need or how they feel.

- **Helpful side**: Problems are out in the open, so they can be solved instead of hidden.
- **Challenge**: Quick words said in anger might cause hurt, especially if the other person is sensitive. Aries might need to pause before speaking during tense moments.

## 4. Loyalty and Defending Loved Ones

When Aries cares about someone, they often defend that person. If they see a loved one insulted, they might speak up right away. They may have no fear about getting involved if they believe someone is acting unfairly toward their partner or best friend. This can create a strong sense of safety for the person they love.

- **Helpful side**: It can be comforting to know Aries will stand up for you, no matter what.

- **Challenge**: Aries might jump into arguments too fast, which can lead to even bigger conflicts.

## 5. Need for Independence

Even though Aries can be caring, they still like having time for themselves. In a close bond, they might want the freedom to follow personal interests, sports, or hobbies. This can confuse a partner who thinks that being close means always being together. Aries might need space to explore their own ideas.

- **Helpful side**: Aries often remain interesting to their partners because they have personal goals and do not lose themselves in the bond.
- **Challenge**: If the other person needs more togetherness, they might feel Aries is pulling away. Balance is important here.

## 6. Handling Disagreements

Every close bond has disagreements. Aries people might show anger strongly, then calm down quickly. They might have a short but intense burst of frustration. If the partner or friend can stay calm, they will see that Aries often feels better soon. The sign's direct nature can help solve issues promptly. However, if both sides get heated, the conflict could become bigger than it needs to be.

- **Helpful side**: Aries' anger, though hot, can be brief. They do not tend to hold grudges for very long.
- **Challenge**: Those few minutes of strong temper might scare or upset someone who fears confrontation. Aries may need to practice gentle ways of expressing hurt.

## 7. Showing Affection

Aries might show affection in ways that match their active energy. They may give playful hugs, quick pecks on the cheek, or silly surprises. They might take a loved one out for a fun game or plan a small but direct gesture, like leaving a note that says, "You mean a lot to me." Because Aries is not always the most subtle sign, their forms of affection can be big or sudden.

- **Helpful side**: These bright displays can lift the other person's spirits and feel exciting.
- **Challenge**: If the other person values slow, quiet moments, the Aries style might feel overwhelming or too spontaneous.

## 8. Encouraging Loved Ones

Aries likes to see people succeed. In a close bond, they might cheer someone on in their projects, sports, or studies. They do not like to sit still if they can give a friendly push. A loved one might hear, "Go for it! I believe you can do it!" from an Aries who is ready to back them up.

- **Helpful side**: Encouragement from an energetic Aries can boost confidence.
- **Challenge**: Aries might try to force a person to do more than they feel ready for. If the other person wants a slower approach, Aries might grow impatient.

## 9. Handling Jealousy

Some Aries may feel jealous if they sense their close friend or partner is giving too much attention to someone else. This can come from Aries' strong emotions. An Aries might say, "I don't like how you spend so much time with that person." This open statement can lead to quick talks about trust. While not every Aries acts jealous, those who do might find it flares up suddenly.

- **Helpful side**: Because Aries is direct, they might talk about jealousy right away instead of letting it silently grow.
- **Challenge**: They can become angry or protective if they feel threatened, which can upset the relationship if not handled calmly.

## 10. Excitement in the Long Term

Aries can bring a sense of fun and renewal even in longer bonds. They might suggest new ideas for date nights, fresh projects, or unexpected trips. This can keep a relationship from becoming dull. However, Aries might lose interest if they feel nothing is happening. To stay steady, they might learn to enjoy quieter days too.

- **Helpful side**: The spark of Aries can make everyday life feel a little more fun and adventurous.
- **Challenge**: If the partner wants peace and a slow routine, Aries might feel bored. Good communication about needs is key.

## 11. Respect for Each Other's Strengths

Aries often likes to be in charge, but they can respect a partner who has their own strong points. For instance, if the partner is good at planning or saving money, Aries might gladly say, "You handle that part, and I'll handle this part." This works best when both sides admit each other's strengths instead of fighting over control.

- **Helpful side**: The pair can become a strong team. Each brings something different to the table.
- **Challenge**: If Aries tries to make every decision alone, the other person might feel ignored or unvalued.

## 12. Trust and Honesty

In any close bond, trust and honesty are vital. Aries generally prefers to lay things out in the open. If Aries has made a mistake, they might admit it (though some Aries can be stubborn before they do). If a partner or friend is not honest, Aries can become angry or disappointed. Direct honesty tends to be something Aries both gives and expects in return.

- **Helpful side**: Problems have less room to fester since everything is talked about.
- **Challenge**: Aries' direct nature might scare someone who is used to hiding problems or feelings.

## 13. Aries and Different Personalities

Aries might bond well with people who enjoy action and lively discussions. A calm and patient person, however, can also suit Aries, because they can bring balance to the Aries' energy. In friendships, an Aries might thrive with pals who like new experiences, but they might also learn from a friend who is more careful and reflective. The key is respect. If Aries respects the differences, there can be a great blend of energies.

- **Helpful side**: Aries can learn patience, while the calmer person can learn spontaneity.
- **Challenge**: Conflict arises if one side feels forced to adopt the other person's style instead of finding middle ground.

## 14. Taking Responsibility

In a close bond, responsibilities appear. Aries might need to learn that not every task is fun or exciting. Bills must be paid on time, chores must be done, and long-term planning matters. Some Aries do well with these tasks, but others might resist them because they crave action. If the bond is important, Aries might find the motivation to handle these tasks so that the relationship stays strong.

- **Helpful side**: Once Aries sets a goal (like making a relationship flourish), they might push themselves to do the less exciting tasks as part of that goal.
- **Challenge**: They may need gentle reminders or a clear plan to stay consistent with routine tasks.

## 15. Balancing Warmth and Personal Freedom

Aries can be warm, hugging someone or expressing devotion, but then suddenly they might say, "I need to go do my own thing." This shift can be confusing for the other person. It is not that Aries stops caring; it is just that their independence is popping up again. Learning to give reassurance—such as saying, "I love you, and I also need a few hours by myself"—can help.

- **Helpful side**: When Aries returns from personal time, they often come back with renewed energy for the bond.
- **Challenge**: If the other person takes it personally, they might feel unloved when Aries needs space.

## 16. Aries in a Serious Relationship

As things get more serious, Aries can still bring excitement. They might plan an event for the two of them or work on a shared project. Aries often invests energy in making the relationship feel active. Some Aries become quite protective and proud of their partner, wanting to show them off to friends or family. They may also want to tackle large plans together—like moving to a new home or reorganizing their shared space.

- **Helpful side**: The relationship can keep a sense of aliveness even as it matures.
- **Challenge**: If Aries gets restless, they might complain about feeling stuck, leading to arguments if they do not talk things out.

## 17. Ending Unhealthy Bonds

Aries might leave a bond if they feel it no longer makes sense. Because they value honesty, they may say, "This isn't working," rather than pretend everything is okay. While that can be painful for everyone involved, it can also be less confusing than a long, quiet drift apart. Aries prefers clear action over slow, hidden problems. Of course, some Aries might try to fix things first, but if that fails, they are not likely to remain in a situation they see as unfair or unhappy.

- **Helpful side**: Quick, clear endings can be healthier than dragging out conflicts for months.
- **Challenge**: The other person might feel rushed if they were hoping to fix things with more time.

## 18. Aries' Own Needs vs. the Bond

Aries might sometimes struggle with the line between personal wants and the needs of the bond. For example, an Aries might want to start a new hobby that takes up many hours a week, while the partner wants more shared time. Aries must learn to balance the two. Close bonds work best when both sides get enough attention and care.

- **Helpful side**: Aries can show the other person that following one's passion can bring fresh energy into the bond.
- **Challenge**: If Aries never makes time for the partner's needs, resentment might build.

# 19. Communication Tips

1. **Share Feelings Calmly**: When emotions run hot, Aries can benefit from taking a moment to breathe before speaking.
2. **Offer Reassurance**: Aries can say, "I'm here for you," or "I do care," especially if the other person seems uneasy about Aries' need for space.
3. **Listen Carefully**: Aries should give the other person a chance to speak fully, without interrupting.
4. **Discuss Goals Together**: Aries can talk about shared hopes or plans, making sure both sides are heard.
5. **Respect Boundaries**: Aries can be enthusiastic, but they should check in to be sure the other person is comfortable with the pace.

# 20. Overall Picture of Aries in Close Bonds

Aries brings brightness, honesty, and a protective spirit to relationships. They can be loyal, standing up for their loved ones when needed. They are quick to express excitement and can make life feel adventurous for their partner or close friend. However, they also need their personal freedom and might have moments of frustration when things move too slowly or feel too controlled. By learning patience and kindness in their words, Aries can build happy, long-lasting bonds.

In the end, an Aries does best when they see a relationship as a teamwork of two (or more, in the case of close friendships). Each person has different needs. Aries can handle tasks that call for bold moves or quick energy, but they should also let the other person shine where they are strong. With honest talk, thoughtful actions, and mutual respect, Aries can have strong and loving connections that spark joy for everyone involved.

# CHAPTER 6: ARIES THROUGH HISTORY

Aries is known today as the first sign of the zodiac, but people have held many ideas about Aries through the ages. In this chapter, we will look at how ancient groups, astrologers in different eras, and modern thinkers have talked about Aries. While we touched briefly on myths in Chapter 2, here we will focus more on the progression of beliefs about Aries and how these ideas changed or stayed the same through time. We will also see how Aries was used as a marker in calendars and in social or cultural settings.

## 1. Ancient Observers of the Sky

Many ancient peoples looked to the night sky for important signs about when to plant crops or perform certain tasks. They noticed that around the beginning of spring in the northern half of the world, the Sun appeared in front of a certain cluster of stars. This cluster, faint but noticeable, became known as Aries. Because spring was so important for planting and warmer weather, these stars took on a special role.

- In **Mesopotamia** (an old region around modern-day Iraq), people saw the stars of Aries and might have connected them with important seasonal points. They studied the skies to understand time and the best moments for agriculture.
- In **ancient Egypt**, priests tracked the rising and setting of constellations. Aries was likely noted, but it was not as famous as some Egyptian star groups. Still, the link of a ram with fertility can be found in Egyptian art, such as with ram-headed gods.

## 2. The Babylonians and Aries

The Babylonians played a major part in forming the zodiac we know. They divided the sky into twelve sections, each with a constellation. Aries was one of them, though it might not have been called Aries at first. Some sources suggest it was referred to as the "Hired Man" or another title. Over time, the symbol of the ram rose in prominence.

- **Why a ram?** Early shapes in the sky might have looked like horns, or they might have matched certain cultural ideas about strong animals.
- **Role in time-keeping**: The Babylonians used the stars to measure months and seasons. Aries was part of that system, helping them keep track of the Sun's path.

## 3. Greek and Roman Influence

The ancient Greeks adopted parts of the Babylonian system and added their own myths, such as the golden ram's tale. They named the constellation Krios (Greek for "ram"). Later, the Romans took much of Greek culture and renamed the gods, but they kept Aries as an important zodiac sign. The Roman calendar started the new year in March in earlier times, which was close to when the Sun moved into Aries. This gave Aries a link to new starts.

- **Greek astronomy**: People like Eudoxus and Ptolemy wrote about the constellations. Aries was described in star catalogs, and it was placed in the sky near Pisces and Taurus.
- **Roman astronomy**: While the Romans did not add many new myths to Aries, they continued using it as part of their astrological and astronomical records.

## 4. Aries in the Middle Ages

In the Middle Ages, astrology was linked closely to medicine and daily life in parts of Europe. Astrologers believed that the zodiac signs could affect health, farming, and even predictions about events in kingdoms. Aries, as the first sign, was seen as a symbol of beginnings. Books called "almanacs" included sections about when the Sun entered Aries and how it might affect plants or people.

- **Medical beliefs**: Some medieval doctors used astrology to decide the best time for treatments. Aries was linked to the head (as each zodiac sign was thought to rule a part of the body). Doctors might have avoided certain procedures during times they believed were ruled by Aries.
- **Farming**: Farmers might have planned planting schedules based on the seasons. Since Aries was connected to spring, it became a sign that people watched for changes in the weather and in the sky.

## 5. Renaissance and the Rise of Modern Science

During the Renaissance in Europe, people began to question old ideas and investigate the world more with observation. Astronomy grew as a science, and the zodiac, including Aries, was studied more carefully. Famous astronomers like Copernicus and Galileo changed how we see the Solar System. Still, astrology remained popular in many courts and among common folks.

- **Charts and star maps**: Artists drew detailed charts of the constellations. Aries was often shown as a ram with curled horns, though the actual stars might not look much like a real ram.
- **Astrology's status**: While astronomy and astrology parted ways in modern science, many people still read horoscopes

or consulted astrologers. Aries continued to be seen as a sign of boldness and action.

## 6. Eastern Views of Aries

In some Asian traditions, the zodiac is different. For example, in Chinese astrology, there is a 12-year cycle of animals, which does not match the Western zodiac. Still, contact between East and West led some Eastern astrologers to know about the Western zodiac system. Aries, in that system, might not hold the same place as it does in the West, but the concept of a ram or sheep can appear in various Eastern stories too (though not always tied to the same dates or meaning).

- **Difference in star grouping**: Some ancient Chinese star maps grouped the Aries stars differently. They did not see them as a ram but as other figures.
- **Modern times**: Today, many in Eastern countries who follow Western astrology see Aries as a sign starting in late March, just as Westerners do, even though it is not part of traditional Eastern systems.

## 7. Aries in Cultural Festivals (Historical Context)

In older European traditions, the time around late March was linked to various events marking the end of winter. Because Aries was visible in the sky and the Sun was entering Aries, people might have performed spring-related customs. While this was not always called an "Aries event," the timing often overlapped with the sign.

- **Seasonal link**: Aries season was near the time of spring's arrival, so it became a convenient marker for the renewal of life in many regions.

- **Use in local calendars**: Some local calendars used the start of Aries as a sign to begin counting certain days or to note that the growing season was near.

## 8. Astrology in the Age of Exploration

As ships traveled around the world in the 15th to 17th centuries, European ideas about astrology and the zodiac, including Aries, went to other continents. Sailors navigated by the stars, though they cared more about star positions for directions than zodiac sign meanings. Still, the concept of Aries as a zodiac sign spread further.

- **Encounter with new skies**: People in the southern half of the world saw different star arrangements. Aries is still visible from many places, but not always in the same shape or at the same time of year.
- **Influence on local beliefs**: In some places, local cultures had their own star stories. The introduction of Aries as "the ram" from Europe added a new layer to these places' sky lore.

## 9. 18th and 19th Century Views

During the 1700s and 1800s, astrology was not as respected among scientists. However, it stayed popular in some circles. Newspapers and almanacs printed short readings for each zodiac sign. Aries was usually described as spirited, bold, and linked to Mars.

- **Planetary connection**: Mars, known as the Red Planet, was often called the ruler of Aries. This link was repeated in many texts, where Aries was said to take on the strong traits of Mars.
- **Cultural references**: Writers and poets sometimes referenced Aries to signal new beginnings or the arrival of spring. The ram became a symbol of forward push in some literary works.

## 10. Modern Western Astrology

In the 20th century, astrology had a surge in mainstream culture, especially in newspapers, magazines, and, later, websites. Aries was still shown as the first sign, and people born between about March 21 and April 19 were labeled Aries. Certain catchphrases—like "dynamic," "courageous," or "energetic"—were repeated in horoscopes. While many read these for fun, others took them more seriously.

- **Personal birth charts**: People began looking beyond their Sun sign (Aries, Taurus, etc.) to find their Moon sign, Ascendant, and other factors. Aries in one's chart could show where a person might show bold traits.
- **Horoscopes**: Aries horoscopes in magazines often talked about leadership, new projects, or strong will. While some see horoscopes as mere entertainment, others believe they hold real insight.

## 11. Aries in Popular Media

Television shows, movies, and books sometimes feature characters who are labeled as Aries to show certain traits. The audience can spot the sign references if they pay close attention. In some animated series or novels, a character might wear a ram symbol or mention being born under Aries. This can hint that the character is energetic, outspoken, or brave.

- **Influence on character design**: Anime or comics might show a ram horn symbol when a hero has Aries-like qualities.
- **Songs and cultural references**: Some artists mention zodiac signs, including Aries, in their work to point out personality hints or new beginnings.

## 12. Aries in Astrology Groups

There are modern astrology groups that meet to discuss each sign's traits, do group readings, or teach about how to draw birth charts. When Aries is the topic, they might go over how to handle Aries energy in everyday life, or how to plan tasks when the Sun is in Aries each year.

- **Seasonal cycles**: Some astrologers note that, in the northern half of the world, Aries season is linked to fresh energy, matching the idea of Aries as a sign of bold starts.
- **Workshops and lessons**: People interested in self-awareness might focus on Aries themes in spring, such as forming new goals, taking action, and being brave.

## 13. Scientific Community's View

From a strictly scientific view, Aries is simply a group of stars with no special power over humans' lives. Astronomers note that, due to the shift in Earth's axis (called precession), the Sun no longer aligns with the same Aries stars during Aries season as it did in ancient times. This difference is called sidereal vs. tropical astrology. However, many Western astrologers still use the tropical system, linking Aries with the spring equinox in the north.

- **Tropical system**: Western astrology sets Aries at the March equinox, around March 20 or 21, ignoring the actual star positions.
- **Sidereal system**: Some Eastern or Vedic traditions try to keep astrology tied to the real star positions, meaning the Sun might not be in Aries on the same dates as the tropical system states.

## 14. Use of Aries in Symbolism

Beyond astrology, the ram symbol has appeared in logos, team mascots, or other designs. This does not always refer to astrology directly, but it still carries that idea of strength, boldness, and leadership. You might see a sports team with a ram symbol, hinting at courage or force.

- **Military or sports**: Some groups use the ram to show power.
- **Schools or clubs**: They might pick the ram to represent forward action, matching the Aries spirit.

## 15. Aries and Modern Psychologists

Some psychologists who explore personality might see value in certain zodiac traits as a way people talk about themselves. Aries, with its talk of leadership and bravery, can be a framework for self-reflection. Though mainstream psychology does not treat astrology as science, it might acknowledge that the zodiac can give people language to describe their traits.

- **Self-awareness**: Someone who identifies with Aries might look at their own habits and say, "I do love starting things," or "I can be blunt."
- **Limits**: Psychologists also note that labeling oneself too strongly can ignore the many other factors that shape us, such as upbringing, environment, and personal choices.

## 16. Aries in Different Spiritual Paths

Some spiritual paths outside the mainstream also embrace the zodiac. Aries might be viewed as a gate of new energy, the spark of life, or a symbol of cosmic fire. People in these groups might perform special activities (like lighting candles or focusing on bold intentions) during Aries season.

- **Fire element**: Many see Aries as connected to the element of fire, which can signify willpower, energy, and bright warmth.
- **Ritual uses**: If a spiritual group aligns with Western astrology, they might do special meditations or group discussions when the Sun enters Aries, using it as a symbol of action.

## 17. Traditional Crafts and Aries

In older times, some crafts tied their tasks to the zodiac. For instance, a group of weavers might say Aries season is time to begin certain patterns. A blacksmith might say that the fiery nature of Aries is perfect for forging iron. Although these traditions were not always consistent, they highlight how people used zodiac symbols to give meaning to their work.

- **Link to sheep's wool**: Aries, being a ram, sometimes led to a link with sheep. In places with sheep farming, folks might have joked about Aries season being the best for shearing sheep (though the actual timing depends on the region).
- **Community beliefs**: Small villages might have had local sayings about Aries, though these are not always well-documented.

## 18. Shifting Meanings Over Time

As centuries passed, the meaning of Aries shifted in small ways. Early on, it was simply a group of stars marking spring. Later, it became the ram of myths. In the Middle Ages, it was part of medical and farming astrology. In modern times, it is both a popular Sun sign in daily horoscopes and a symbol in personal growth talks.

- **Common thread**: The idea of new beginnings runs through nearly all the stages. Aries is consistently linked to a fresh start, either in farming, in the zodiac, or in personal life.

- **Different emphasis**: Some eras saw Aries mostly as a star sign for navigation or time-keeping, while others treated it as a source of personality traits and daily guidance.

## 19. Aries in Present-Day Culture

Today, Aries remains a well-known sign in Western astrology. Many people, even those who are not deeply into astrology, know that Aries is the "first sign" or that Aries folks can be quite energetic. The symbol of the ram appears in everything from greeting cards to social media posts. Some use Aries as a shorthand for people who are quick to act.

- **Online communities**: Social media has countless groups or pages where users post Aries memes or jokes, highlighting how an Aries might react in funny situations.
- **Fashion and accessories**: Some brands sell necklaces or bracelets with the Aries symbol for those who want to show their zodiac identity.

## 20. The Enduring Legacy of Aries

From its ancient roots in Babylonian star lore to modern social media memes, Aries has had a long and varied history. Though science and astronomy might not support the idea that Aries shapes our fates, millions of people still find meaning in the ram's bold energy. The sign stands for a push forward, a spark of energy, and the spirit of "let's go!" that many people find uplifting. Whether in old stories of the golden ram or in a brand-new horoscope post online, Aries stays a sign that people link with new starts and bright courage.

Looking over the centuries, we see Aries consistently tied to the sense of spring, fresh life, and eagerness. In older days, it helped mark time and seasons, guiding farmers and early astronomers. In the medieval and Renaissance eras, it carried both practical advice (about health or planting) and mythic meaning. Today, it is part of pop culture, personal identity, and discussions about personality.

For those interested in astrology, Aries stands as a sign of directness, boldness, and warmth—qualities that can energize life when used well. From a historical view, Aries shows how humans have always looked to the sky for meaning and placed our hopes and stories among the stars. While the specific tales and uses vary over time, the lasting image of the ram reminds us of the spark of life returning each year in spring, a symbol that continues to shine in the night sky for those who seek it.

# CHAPTER 7: ARIES & CONFIDENCE

Aries is often linked to self-assurance and a bold way of dealing with life. While not every Aries will show complete certainty all the time, many Aries folks do tend to feel strong enough to tackle new tasks or speak up for themselves. In this chapter, we will explore the idea of Aries and confidence: where it comes from, how it shows up, and what challenges can arise. We will also look at ways Aries might handle self-doubt or criticism, and how they can use their natural boldness in a balanced way.

## 1. Early Signs of Confidence

Many Aries children show signs of bravery early on. They might be the first to climb a tall slide or speak up in class. This can come from a natural push to try things without worrying too much about what might go wrong. Other kids might ask, "What if I fall?" but the Aries child might think, "Let's see how high I can climb!" This kind of outlook can lead to quick learning and a willingness to grab at new chances. Yet it can also lead to bumps and bruises if the Aries child acts too fast.

- **Upside**: Early boldness can teach important lessons. An Aries child might gain skills sooner than peers because they try things right away.
- **Challenge**: Confidence without caution can cause problems, such as getting hurt or making mistakes that could have been avoided with a slower approach.

## 2. Sources of Aries Confidence

Where does this self-assurance come from? Part of it is linked to the fire element that is often associated with Aries in astrology. Fire can mean warmth, passion, and a spark of courage. Some Aries folks may feel a strong sense of "I can do this," even if they have never tried a task before. Another source is the planet Mars, which is said to rule Aries. Mars is connected to action and assertiveness. In simple terms, Aries often carries that "go for it" attitude that can help them do well in many settings.

- **Desire for action**: Because Aries likes to move and act, they often do not dwell on doubts for too long. They feel the urge to try, rather than sit and worry.
- **Positive self-talk**: Some Aries naturally use hopeful words with themselves, like "Let's go!" or "Yes, I can!" This inner voice can be a strong motivator.

## 3. Expressing Confidence in Public

Aries confidence can show up plainly when they are around other people. They might speak in a firm tone, stand up straight, or stride into a room ready to get things done. In group settings like classes or clubs, an Aries might raise a hand first to answer a question or volunteer for a task. This can be inspiring to others who feel shy about speaking. It can also, however, make some people see Aries as too pushy, especially if Aries does not take time to listen to everyone.

- **Helpful side**: People often look up to an Aries who steps forward. This can make Aries a natural leader in groups or activities.
- **Potential issue**: If Aries always steps forward, others might not get a chance. Aries could learn to share tasks or let someone else speak first.

## 4. Balancing Confidence and Humility

Real confidence does not mean ignoring other people's ideas or feelings. Sometimes, Aries folks might slip into overconfidence if they get too carried away by the idea that they can do anything. Overconfidence can lead them to miss useful advice or warnings. An Aries might say, "I know best," and move ahead alone, not realizing that teamwork or guidance could have helped avoid trouble.

- **Why balance matters**: True self-assurance means believing in oneself but also recognizing that everyone has more to learn.
- **Ways to stay balanced**: Aries can pause to ask questions, gather feedback from others, or do a bit of research before acting. This does not kill their spark but makes it safer and wiser.

## 5. Handling Criticism

Even the most self-assured Aries can face moments when someone criticizes their work or decisions. Because Aries invests energy and heart into things, they can feel hurt or annoyed when someone points out flaws. They might react with anger ("You do not understand!") or try to defend themselves strongly, even if the critique was meant to be helpful. Learning to handle criticism well is a big step toward healthy self-confidence. Instead of viewing negative feedback as an attack, Aries can see it as a chance to improve.

- **Practical tips**:
  1. **Take a breath** before replying. A quick reaction might lead to arguments.
  2. **Listen fully** to what the other person says. Sometimes, there is good information hidden in the critique.

3. **Decide what applies**. Not all criticism is fair or useful. Aries can pick out what is helpful and let go of the rest.
4. **Reply calmly** with thanks for the feedback if it was given kindly. This shows real self-assurance.

## 6. Building Confidence in School or Work

In a school setting, Aries might shine in subjects where action or hands-on work is needed. They might enjoy sports, debates, drama, or science experiments. Their confidence can also appear in group projects if they feel they can lead. However, they might stumble in tasks that require long, careful study with little excitement. Keeping confidence in these areas might require new strategies.

- **Ideas for Aries**:
    - Set small goals to stay motivated.
    - Work with a study buddy who can share calm methods, which can help Aries slow down and notice details.
    - Use that boldness to ask questions in class rather than get bored.

In the workplace, Aries might do well in roles that let them solve problems or start new things. They often like having a sense of movement in their job. Confidence helps them speak up in meetings or pitch ideas to the boss. However, if the job demands lots of quiet, repetitive tasks, an Aries might get restless or lose confidence in their ability to stay focused. Finding ways to keep the spark alive is key.

## 7. Facing Self-Doubt

Believe it or not, Aries people can experience self-doubt. Sometimes, they hide it with a show of being overly bold. For instance, if an Aries fails at something they really cared about, they might act like they do not care at all. Yet deep down, they might wonder if they are good enough. Recognizing these feelings is important. True confidence includes accepting that everyone has weak spots and can learn from them.

- **How Aries can face doubt**:
    - **Reflect on strengths**: Make a simple list of what they do well.
    - **Learn from mistakes**: Ask, "What can I do better next time?" instead of saying, "I never fail!"
    - **Talk to a trusted friend**: Aries might open up to someone who can give calm, honest feedback.

## 8. Aries and Group Confidence

Aries does not have to shine alone. Sometimes, the strongest confidence an Aries can show is helping the whole group feel brave. If Aries sees group members uncertain, Aries might say, "We can do this, let's try!" This group confidence can be a powerful tool in solving challenges or building team spirit. Others might admire Aries for bringing them out of their shells.

- **Sharing the spotlight**: The best Aries leaders do not hog all the attention. They share tasks and praise so that everyone feels included.
- **Dealing with group pushback**: If a group is not ready to move as fast as Aries wants, Aries can practice patience and break tasks into steps the group can handle.

## 9. Physical Confidence

Because Aries is often linked to energy, many Aries folks enjoy physical activities—sports, dancing, running, martial arts, and so on. They might feel confident pushing their bodies to perform. This can build even more self-assurance, as physical success (like finishing a race) can remind Aries that they are capable of growth.

- **Upside**: Success in a favorite sport or exercise plan can boost self-esteem.
- **Challenge**: If Aries compares themselves too strongly to others, they might feel upset on days they do not perform well. Learning to accept that not every day is a winning day is part of healthy confidence.

## 10. Confidence in Conversation

Aries can show a lot of spirit in simple chats. They might talk with passion about their hobbies or ideas. This can be fun for friends, who see the excitement shining out. Still, Aries must watch out for dominating the conversation or dismissing others' viewpoints too quickly. Real confidence means feeling secure enough to hear out different opinions.

- **Tips for healthy talks**:
    1. **Practice active listening**: Aries can nod, ask questions, and show genuine curiosity about what the other person says.
    2. **Wait for a pause**: Aries might hold back a second or two before replying, ensuring the other person finished speaking.
    3. **Offer respect**: Even if Aries disagrees, they can say, "I see your point, though I feel differently," instead of dismissing it as wrong.

## 11. Dealing with Peer Pressure

Confident Aries people might not be as affected by peer pressure as some others, because they tend to stand firm in their own choices. However, there can be moments when the crowd's opinion conflicts with Aries' wishes. Aries might feel torn between going with the group or keeping their personal stance. In these times, their natural boldness can help them say, "I'm sorry, but I don't agree," or "I want to do it my way."

- **Sticking to personal values**: If Aries believes something is right, they often will not bend just to fit in. This can be a sign of true moral courage.
- **Being open-minded**: At the same time, Aries can consider whether they are pushing back just to be contrary. True confidence is also flexible when it sees real merit in other people's suggestions.

## 12. Overcoming Setbacks

Confidence can take a hit when Aries faces a big failure, such as losing a job, failing a test, or not succeeding in a contest. Aries might feel frustrated that their usual spark did not lead to a quick fix. During these times, they might blame themselves or blame circumstances in anger. A healthier path is to treat setbacks as temporary. Aries can say, "Yes, I stumbled, but I can stand up again and do better."

- **Actions for recovery**:
    - **Review what went wrong**. Did Aries rush, skip details, or lack needed info?
    - **Plan small improvements**. Make changes step by step rather than trying to fix everything at once.
    - **Use that inner push**. Remind themselves of how many times they have tackled new goals successfully.

## 13. Confidence at Different Life Stages

- **Childhood**: Aries kids might show a fearless side, but parents should guide them on safety and respect for boundaries.

- **Teen years**: Aries teens might push against rules, feeling sure they can handle life. They can learn that advice from elders is not always a block to freedom; it can be a safety net.
- **Adulthood**: Aries adults may keep that spark of boldness, which can help them excel in careers or personal plans. They should, however, watch out for work burnout if they push themselves nonstop.

At each stage, confidence might look different, but the core idea of "I can do this" often remains. Aries can learn to mold that confidence into something wise rather than reckless.

## 14. Healthy Pride vs. Self-Importance

Many Aries folks feel proud of what they do. Healthy pride means being glad about your successes or talents while still remembering that others have their own gifts too. Self-importance is when a person believes they are always better or more worthy. Aries might sometimes slip into self-importance if they do not keep their pride in check.

- **Signs of healthy pride**:

    1. You feel happy about what you have done but also want to help others succeed.
    2. You do not seek to prove you are the best all the time.
    3. You feel gratitude when others help you.
- **Signs of self-importance**:

    1. You ignore others' achievements and focus only on yours.
    2. You get angry if someone else is praised.
    3. You think rules do not apply to you.

## 15. Confidence and Friendships

Aries often brings energy to friendships, whether that means planning outings or starting group chats. Their self-assurance can inspire friends to join events they might have skipped otherwise. However, Aries must be aware of friends who prefer slower or calmer fun. True confidence includes respecting a friend who says, "I'm not in the mood for a big event. Let's do something quiet."

- **Trust-building**: Friends might trust an Aries who is consistent and dependable, not just brave. Confidence also means keeping your word, being on time, and offering honest support.
- **Conflict resolution**: If Aries and a friend clash, confidence can help Aries face the issue quickly. But Aries should also allow the friend time to share their side.

## 16. Symbols of Confidence for Aries

Because Aries is linked to the ram and the color red, some Aries folks might like to wear a small red accent or a ram symbol as a reminder of their bold side. While this is not mandatory, symbols can be helpful for those who enjoy a physical token of self-belief. It might be a bracelet, a small pin, or even a piece of art in their room.

- **Note on balance**: Symbols can spark positivity, but the real work of confidence happens in daily actions, choices, and honest self-talk.

## 17. Aries Confidence in Love or Close Bonds

We have covered Aries in love in an earlier chapter, but here we can note how confidence shapes those bonds. Aries might take the lead in expressing feelings or planning activities with a partner. This can be exciting, but the partner should also have room to share opinions or lead at times. Confidence in a bond means trusting that love does not require constant control. Instead, it thrives on mutual respect and shared happiness.

- **Listening in close bonds**: True confidence lets Aries hear a partner's thoughts without feeling threatened.
- **Apologizing when needed**: If Aries messed up, a confident Aries can say, "I'm sorry," rather than pretend nothing happened.

## 18. Using Confidence to Help Others

Confident Aries people can be valuable to friends, family, or neighbors who struggle with fear or hesitation. For example, Aries might help someone practice for a speech, using encouraging words. Or they might invite a shy person to join a fun outing, gently helping them feel included. By giving support, Aries also grows in empathy and learns that confidence is not just about personal gain but about lifting others too.

- **Ways to help**:
    - Offering to stand with someone who is nervous (like at a talent show).
    - Sharing tips on how to speak up.
    - Reminding others of their strengths.

## 19. Staying Grounded

Confidence can open doors, but Aries should watch for signs that they are becoming so sure they forget to prepare. For example, if they have a big test or a performance, simply believing they will do great does not replace studying or practice. Staying grounded means keeping that spark alive while also doing the work needed to excel.

- **Checks and balances**:
    1. Make a list of what needs to be done to succeed.
    2. Ask for help or advice from people with more experience.
    3. Review progress from time to time to see if you are on track.

## 20. Summary of Aries Confidence

Aries confidence is often fueled by a natural eagerness to act, a willingness to speak up, and a desire to lead or try new things. When used wisely, it helps Aries stand out as someone who can encourage or guide others, spark creative plans, and overcome obstacles with a "can-do" attitude. Yet this spark needs balance. Overconfidence can create mistakes or hurt relationships if Aries forgets to listen, learn, or respect quieter people.

A truly confident Aries is one who can say, "I believe in myself," while also saying, "I'm open to learning, and I value what others bring too." They handle criticism with grace, own up to mistakes, and keep pushing forward. They do not let setbacks crush them, instead seeing each stumble as a step toward growth. They use their lively spirit to help those around them feel braver. In the end, Aries confidence shines best when it is guided by kindness, respect for others, and a humble acceptance that nobody knows it all.

This approach gives Aries a powerful blend of boldness and wisdom. It allows them to be a shining example of how to trust yourself while staying considerate of the people who share your life.

# CHAPTER 8: ARIES IN DAILY LIFE

Aries is often associated with action and energy, but how does that show up in daily routines? This chapter looks at the everyday habits, choices, and rhythms Aries people might have. We will explore how Aries approaches mornings, chores, work or school tasks, free time, and even digital life. By seeing how Aries acts in normal, day-to-day settings, we can better understand both the joys and the struggles that come from having that fiery spark.

## 1. Morning Routines

Aries folks might either jump out of bed ready to face the day or hit the snooze button a few times if they stayed up late on a project. Many Aries enjoy the idea of starting fresh each morning. They often feel a sense of excitement about what new tasks or fun things might happen. Because they can be energetic, they might like a quick exercise or a quick check of their plans for the day as soon as they wake up.

- **Upside**: Waking up with energy can help an Aries get going fast. They might be the first one out the door.
- **Challenge**: If they are not in the mood or if they had a late night, they might get grumpy in the morning. Rest is just as important as action.

## 2. Planning the Day

Some Aries prefer not to over-plan, feeling that too many lists or schedules slow them down. They might keep a rough idea in their head—"I'll do this first, then that, then see what comes up." Others might enjoy short checklists because it can be satisfying to cross items off quickly. The main point is that Aries often likes to stay flexible in case new opportunities pop up.

- **Possible style**:
    - Start with the biggest task of the day while energy is high.
    - Tackle problems right away rather than waiting.
    - Leave space for something fun or unexpected.
- **Potential pitfall**: Skipping detailed planning can lead to forgetting important details. Aries might need a reminder system for tasks that are not so exciting.

## 3. Approaching Chores and Responsibilities

Aries can be quick to handle tasks that feel "urgent" or "interesting." For example, if a sink is leaking and water is spilling, Aries might rush to fix it because it is an immediate problem. But chores that do not seem urgent, like tidying up a room, might be ignored until they become a bigger deal. Over time, this can cause clutter or stress.

- **Helpful idea**: Aries can set a timer for short bursts of chores, turning them into a mini-challenge. This way, the task feels more active and less dull.
- **Balance**: If Aries lives with others, they can talk about dividing tasks so no one feels burdened. Aries might handle quick, immediate jobs, while someone else takes on slower, steady chores.

## 4. Daily Energy Swings

Because Aries runs on bursts of energy, they might feel supercharged at certain points and then crash if they do not pace themselves. Some Aries do well with small breaks where they can move around, stretch, or do something active. This recharges their minds. If Aries tries to sit still for long hours, they might grow restless and unfocused.

- **Handling restlessness**:

    - Stand up, take a short walk, or do a quick chore to break up dull tasks.
    - Allow some variety in the day, switching between different activities if possible.
- **Caution**: Too many quick changes can lead to half-finished tasks. Aries needs to find a balance so that they do not jump from one thing to another without completing anything.

## 5. Food and Meal Habits

An Aries might get so caught up in doing stuff that they forget to eat a proper meal, grabbing quick snacks instead. Other Aries love the stimulation of cooking and might try bold recipes if they enjoy being in the kitchen. For daily meals, Aries might choose fast, easy options unless they have a real interest in cooking.

- **Tip for health**: Taking a little time to plan balanced meals can give Aries better energy throughout the day.
- **Fun approach**: Aries could see cooking as a mini adventure by trying new flavors or methods, keeping mealtime exciting.

## 6. Aries at School or Work

On a normal school or work day, Aries often shows enthusiasm for tasks that let them take charge or try new ideas. They might volunteer for a project or quickly start a conversation in a team meeting. They may not enjoy tasks that are repetitive or slow. Still, these tasks can be part of daily life, so finding ways to make them more engaging is key.

- **Thriving in teamwork**: Aries can do well in group projects if they learn to hear other voices. They bring spark and motivation to the table.
- **Handling boredom**: If the work gets dull, Aries might look for small ways to improve it or suggest changes that could speed things up. If that is not possible, Aries might try to complete the task quickly so they can move on to something else.

## 7. Commuting and Travel

If Aries needs to commute, they might handle it in a direct way: get in the car or on the bus and just go. They often do not like to waste time. If traffic is slow, Aries can get frustrated. A calm approach, like listening to upbeat music or an interesting talk, might help them stay patient. Walking or biking (if possible) might also suit Aries, as it adds a bit of physical activity and breaks the boredom of sitting in traffic.

- **Tip for busy Aries**: Plan to leave a bit earlier to avoid the stress of running late. This can help keep frustration down.
- **Balance**: Aries might need to remind themselves that they cannot control traffic or delays. Accepting this can reduce anger.

## 8. Technology and Media in Daily Life

Aries can enjoy gadgets and apps that help them act fast or keep in touch. They might use a phone calendar or reminders to make sure they do not miss an event. On social media, Aries might post updates or photos showing their active days or accomplishments. They may also like lively online communities where they can share opinions or ideas.

- **Possible risk**: Aries might get into heated arguments online if they feel strongly about a topic. Keeping a calm tone can prevent unneeded stress.
- **Healthy habit**: Turning off devices for a short period to rest the mind. Constant alerts can make Aries more restless than necessary.

## 9. Interactions with Others

In daily life, Aries often interacts with many people: coworkers, classmates, neighbors, or service workers. They might bring friendliness to these short meetings, but they can also get impatient if they feel something is taking too long. For example, waiting in a line can annoy an Aries who wants to keep moving.

- **Ways to keep calm**:
    - Use the time to think of a new idea or plan.
    - Practice quick breathing exercises or recall something happy.
    - Chat politely with others in line, turning waiting into a small social moment.
- **Building a good reputation**: Aries who greet others with a smile and treat them kindly, even when in a hurry, can spread a positive image and brighten someone's day.

## 10. Evening Wind-Down

After a day of moving around, Aries might still have a hard time switching off at night. They might want to start new tasks or finish something that excited them earlier. This can push bedtime later and lead to feeling exhausted the next morning. A daily life tip for Aries is to set a relaxing evening routine: maybe a bit of light reading, a warm beverage, or calm music to slow the mind.

- **Helpful routine**:

    1. Turn down bright lights.
    2. Avoid checking phones or computers right before bed, as they can keep the brain active.
    3. Write down tomorrow's to-dos on paper to free the mind from racing thoughts.
- **Importance of sleep**: Aries has plenty of energy, but a tired Aries can become cranky. Getting enough rest helps maintain that bright spirit.

## 11. Aries and Daily Exercise

Many Aries benefit from some form of regular exercise. A brisk walk, a short run, or even a home workout session can let them use up extra energy that might otherwise come out as restlessness or irritation. If Aries has a busy schedule, they might fit in quick exercises whenever possible—like climbing stairs instead of using an elevator.

- **Motivation**: Aries might see exercise as a personal challenge, tracking progress to stay motivated.
- **Variety**: Changing up workouts can prevent boredom and keep Aries excited about staying active.

## 12. Handling Daily Stress

Stress is part of life for everyone. Aries might feel it strongly if they sense their plans or freedom are blocked. Traffic jams, slow decision-making in meetings, or having to wait too long for results can all raise Aries' stress. Some Aries people might get tense shoulders or headaches when stressed. Recognizing these signs early can help them manage stress in healthy ways.

- **Methods to reduce stress**:

- Take a few minutes to breathe slowly.
- Stand up and walk around, if possible, to burn off frustration.
- Talk things over with a friend or coworker to find quick solutions.
- Use humor or a short break to reset.

## 13. Aries' Daily Communication Style

Aries might send texts that are short and direct. They do not always add many details. If they want something, they might simply write, "Let's do this now." They appreciate quick answers. In emails, they might want to get to the point. While some people enjoy short messages, others might find them too abrupt. Aries can learn to add a friendly greeting or a closing line to keep messages warm.

- **Tips for better daily communication**:
    - Start a text or email with a quick "Hello!" or "Hope you're doing well."
    - Close with something like "Thanks" or "Have a good day!" to show courtesy.
    - If Aries is upset, wait before sending a message. A calm approach can prevent misunderstandings.

## 14. Aries and Errands

Errands like grocery shopping or picking up items can feel like a chore for Aries if they are not exciting. Aries might try to finish them quickly so they can move on to fun tasks. They might go through a store at top speed, grabbing what they need. While this is efficient, they might forget items if they rush too much.

- **Helpful trick**: Make a short list of must-have items before heading out. This prevents second trips.

- **Making it fun**: Aries can set a challenge, such as completing the store visit in a certain amount of time, or finding one new interesting snack.

## 15. Daily Interactions with Family or Housemates

Living with an Aries can mean lively talks and quick decisions. They might wake up saying, "Let's rearrange the living room!" This can be fun but also sudden for housemates who prefer planning. Aries often shares stories about the day, sometimes in a high-spirited way.

- **Keeping harmony**:
    - If Aries wants to change something big at home, they can ask others for their opinions first.
    - Aries can help with tasks that require fast action, like running errands or cleaning up a spill right away.
    - For tasks that need slow care (like sorting old boxes), Aries might ask for help or do them in small pieces to avoid boredom.

## 16. Leisure and Relaxation

Aries often looks for fun that involves movement or fresh challenges. This might mean going outdoors, playing sports, or doing a craft that gives quick results. They might not enjoy quiet hobbies that require hours of sitting still. However, some Aries do find joy in calm pastimes if there is a sense of progress or creativity.

- **Examples**:
    - Video games with quick action or puzzle-solving.
    - Short creative projects like painting a small canvas or building a simple model.
    - Fun outings with friends, such as a park visit or a short trip to a nearby attraction.

## 17. Aries and Friend Meetups

When meeting friends after school or work, Aries might pick a place or activity that is lively. They could suggest a new restaurant, a bowling alley, or a simple walk in the city. They like the idea of doing something active rather than just sitting for hours. If their friends prefer quiet chat, Aries may need to compromise by finding a relaxed but not too dull environment.

- **Spur-of-the-moment invites**: Aries might text a friend last-minute to meet up, which can be fun but might not suit a friend who needs more notice.
- **Being flexible**: Aries can learn to sometimes go with calmer plans to bond with friends who have a different pace.

## 18. Evening Hobbies and Screen Time

After finishing chores or school/work tasks, Aries might scroll through social media, watch fast-paced shows, or play energetic games. If they are not careful, they can lose track of time. Setting boundaries helps them get enough sleep. Some Aries might enjoy reading, but usually something that captures their attention right away, such as an exciting tale or an inspiring true story.

- **Idea**: If Aries starts feeling restless in the evening, they could try a short walk or simple stretches to unwind before bedtime.
- **Warning**: Too much screen time can overstimulate an Aries brain, making it harder to relax.

## 19. Aries and Personal Reflection

While Aries might not always think of themselves as reflective, they can still benefit from a few moments of calm to check in with their feelings. A short daily recap—"What went well today? What do I need to fix tomorrow?"—can help them stay on track. This reflection does not need to be long or deep if that feels unnatural. Even a one-minute check can bring clarity.

- **Why it matters**: Aries can see if they hurt someone's feelings, missed an important detail, or forgot a promise. Then they can correct it quickly.
- **Possible method**: Keep a small notebook to jot down one positive and one not-so-great event each day. Over time, this gives a clearer idea of patterns in daily life.

## 20. The Essence of Aries in Daily Life

Aries thrives when each day has a bit of newness, a challenge to solve, or an exciting project to begin. Routine tasks can bore them unless they spice them up. They like to move, make decisions, and interact with others in a straightforward way. Yet they need to watch out for impatience or frustration when things do not go fast enough.

A balanced Aries day might include:

- A brief plan in the morning.
- Time for movement or a fun break in between tasks.
- A sense of achievement by tackling something new or finishing an old task with renewed energy.
- Polite and open chats with others, remembering to hear them out.
- A wind-down period that helps Aries calm their active mind.

By embracing these ideas, Aries can fill everyday life with purpose and excitement without letting the urge for action take over completely. The goal is to keep that spark alive while also handling responsibilities and caring for personal well-being. When they find this balance, Aries individuals can enjoy each day's flow, sharing their bright spirit with everyone around them and ending the day feeling satisfied and eager for what tomorrow might bring.

# CHAPTER 9: GROWING UP AS AN ARIES

Growing up can be a time of discovery, excitement, and change for everyone. When we talk about an Aries child or teenager, some special traits might appear more clearly. Aries has a fiery spirit, a direct way of dealing with problems, and a bright eagerness that can shape many parts of childhood and beyond. In this chapter, we will look at how an Aries might grow from a young child into a teen and later an adult, all while keeping that classic Aries spark. We will also explore the challenges and rewards that can come with having Aries qualities at different ages. Though each individual has unique experiences, we can see patterns in how Aries traits tend to show up over time.

## 1. Aries Infancy and Toddler Years

Babies do not talk about zodiac signs, of course, but parents of Aries infants sometimes notice signs of a bold spirit early on. An Aries baby might:

- **Cry loudly and suddenly** when something is wrong, wanting quick attention or a solution.
- **Be quick to explore** the moment they can crawl or walk, often reaching for new objects or places without fear.
- **Show strong likes and dislikes** (for instance, a certain toy they love to grab or a type of food they instantly reject).

Some caregivers say that Aries toddlers can be energetic, running from one side of the room to the other with big smiles or loud squeals. They might enjoy physical activities like climbing on furniture or jumping around, which can be fun but also risky if no one is watching closely.

**Tips for Caregivers of Aries Infants and Toddlers**

1. **Safe spaces to explore**: Because Aries little ones might dart around, it helps to have a child-friendly area where they can move and play without getting hurt.
2. **Quick response to needs**: Aries kids want to see action. If they are crying or fussing about something, checking on them swiftly can help them feel secure.
3. **Calm but firm limits**: Even if they are small, Aries children can show strong will. Setting simple, clear boundaries helps them learn what is safe or not. Yelling or harsh methods may make them more upset, while calm direction can guide them well.

## 2. Aries in Early Childhood (Ages 4–7)

Once Aries kids reach preschool or early school years, their active side often becomes clearer. Teachers or parents might notice:

- **Eagerness to lead**: An Aries child might volunteer to be the line leader at preschool or want to be the "helper" during class activities.
- **Bold attempts**: They could be the first to try a new piece of playground equipment or the first to raise a hand when the teacher asks a question.
- **Strong feelings**: Aries children might laugh loudly when they are happy, but also cry loudly or get upset quickly if they are frustrated.

During this stage, Aries kids are learning basic skills—counting, reading simple words, playing with others, and more. Their fiery energy can help them jump into these tasks. However, they might also dislike slower, repetitive lessons. They might say, "This is boring," or squirm in their seat if the teacher is repeating the same information many times.

### Social Interactions

- **Making friends**: Aries children often approach other kids directly: "Hi, do you want to play?" This can help them form friendships quickly.
- **Handling conflicts**: If an Aries child disagrees with a classmate, they might shout or act out right away. Learning to talk through problems calmly is an important skill at this age.

### Tips for Adults Working with Aries Kids

1. **Encourage teamwork**: Aries children can do well in small group activities where they learn to share roles.
2. **Offer short tasks**: Breaking a long lesson into smaller, more active parts helps keep them focused.
3. **Use positive language**: Saying, "Look how quickly you tried that puzzle—good effort!" can reinforce their bold attempts while reminding them that it is okay if they do not finish first every time.

## 3. Middle Childhood (Ages 8–11)

As Aries kids grow older, their eagerness might lead them to new interests. They could sign up for sports, music, art, or something else that lets them move or shine. Many Aries children enjoy:

- **Team sports**: They like friendly competition and the chance to run around (soccer, basketball, etc.).
- **Creative clubs**: Some Aries kids love drama class or music lessons, wanting a stage where they can stand out.

- **STEM activities**: Others might enjoy science experiments that involve hands-on work or quick results.

During this period, Aries kids often want more independence. They might insist on packing their own bag for school or choosing their own outfits. This can be helpful if they learn to handle responsibilities early. However, they might get upset if a parent tries to do things for them without asking. Aries kids like to feel they can do it themselves.

**Emotional Growth**

- **Learning about patience**: An Aries child might find it hard to wait their turn. Helping them see the value of patience can be a big lesson.
- **Dealing with frustration**: If a project does not go smoothly, Aries might want to give up or storm off. Supportive adults can show them that taking a break, then coming back to the task, can lead to success.

**School Life**

- **Participation in class**: Aries kids might answer questions quickly, even if they are not fully sure, because they love being involved. Teachers can harness that enthusiasm but also encourage them to think before speaking.
- **Completing homework**: If they find a subject dull, Aries kids may rush through assignments or forget them. Making homework into a timed challenge or focusing on short sessions might help.

## 4. Aries in Early Teens (Ages 12–14)

The teenage years can be tricky for anyone, and for Aries, the changes in body and mind can be extra intense. Aries teens might:

- **Want freedom**: They could ask for more independence than before, wanting to pick their own activities or see friends without constant limits.
- **Show strong opinions**: If they do not like a rule, they can say so plainly, sometimes leading to arguments with parents or teachers.
- **Explore identity**: Aries teens might try out new looks or hobbies, searching for what feels right to them.

Social life becomes bigger in these years. Aries teens may either be quite popular because of their outgoing nature or might clash with peers if they come across as pushy. Learning to listen and cooperate becomes vital.

## Common Teen Challenges

1. **Mood changes**: Aries can shift from excited to grumpy if they feel something is not fair. Teen hormones can add to these swings.
2. **Peer pressure**: Confident Aries might resist peer pressure, but if they do give in, it could be because they want action or excitement.
3. **Authority conflicts**: Teachers or parents who use strict commands without explanation might face pushback from Aries teens who ask, "Why should I?"

## Positive Outlets for Aries Teens

- **Sports and clubs**: Physical activities can help them burn off energy and build teamwork skills.
- **Creative arts**: Theater, dance, or music can channel their passion.
- **Leadership roles**: Roles like class representative or team captain can give them a sense of purpose and responsibility.

# 5. Late Teens (Ages 15–18)

In the later teen years, Aries might start thinking more about their future. Some Aries teens have big dreams—they might talk about what they want to do after school or what kind of path they hope to follow. Their natural eagerness can be a strength, motivating them to apply to colleges, join training programs, or learn a trade. On the other hand, they may also worry if they are not sure which path to take, because they dislike feeling stuck.

- **Possible Achievements**: Aries teens who have found a passion can excel in it, whether it is sports, academics, arts, or something else. They like feeling they are moving forward.
- **Potential Pitfalls**: If they have not found a strong interest, they might feel restless and act out. They might change plans several times, trying to find something that truly excites them.

## Relationships and Independence

- **Friends and romance**: Aries might enter close bonds with a bold and open approach. They may show strong feelings quickly, which can be thrilling but sometimes overwhelming for others.
- **Family ties**: These can be tested if the Aries teen wants more space. Calm talks where each side listens can help reduce conflicts.
- **Decision-making**: Aries might want to make big decisions alone. However, seeking advice from trusted adults can guide them to think about pros and cons.

## 6. Aries Entering Adulthood (Ages 19–24)

As Aries steps into early adulthood, the wish for freedom and the desire to do something meaningful can guide many choices. Some Aries young adults might:

- **Jump into higher education**: They may pick fields that let them act or lead. They could stand out in student clubs or teams.
- **Look for a job**: Aries might be drawn to roles with action—sales, events, marketing, or something hands-on. They prefer not to be stuck in a quiet corner.
- **Travel or explore new places**: Aries often likes to see new sights and test themselves in different settings.

This phase can feel exciting but also uncertain. Aries might want fast progress. If they do not see results, they can get frustrated. Patience is still a lesson many Aries must keep learning. On the bright side, their energy and boldness can lead them to fun opportunities, new friends, or new ideas.

## 7. Aries in the Mid-20s to 30s

By this stage, many Aries have found some form of path—though it might change a few times. Aries can do well if they choose work that taps into their energy, be it running a small business, engaging in creative arts, or working in a fast-paced environment. Some Aries might thrive in leadership roles, while others prefer being free agents, not tied to a boss.

### Friendships and Bonds

- **Solid social circles**: Aries likely has a group of friends who appreciate their direct manner. Aries remains loyal and often fun to be around.

- **Relationships**: If Aries enters a serious bond, they bring warmth and defense of their loved ones. They also need space to follow their personal dreams, so a balance is important.

**Career Growth**

- **Boldness at work**: Aries might propose ideas in meetings, volunteer for projects, or handle tasks that scare others.
- **Challenges**: Overconfidence can be a risk. Aries must learn to plan carefully, not only rely on spur-of-the-moment decisions.
- **Learning curve**: Taking feedback without anger can help Aries improve quickly and earn respect from coworkers.

## 8. Aries in the 30s and 40s

By their 30s or 40s, Aries often has a clearer sense of who they are. They might have a job that matches their need for action or variety. Some Aries could also be parents, applying their natural energy to family life. Even though Aries at this age is more mature, that spark may still appear in the urge to try new projects or experiences.

- **Family Life**: As parents, Aries might be playful and spontaneous. They often encourage kids to be bold and try new things. Sometimes, though, patience is needed when kids do not move as quickly as Aries expects.
- **Career Shifts**: Aries might pivot if they feel stuck. Changing roles or starting a business can happen. They do not like routines that have lost their purpose.
- **Emotional Growth**: Over the years, Aries might have learned to pause before reacting, which can lessen conflicts. However, that fiery heart is still there, ready to defend loved ones or push forward when needed.

## 9. Aries in the 50s and Beyond

As Aries grows older, they might still hold onto that sense of excitement. Many Aries seniors stay active, continuing to learn new skills or engage in physical activities as much as their health allows. They might:

- **Join community groups**: Aries can share knowledge, lead events, or mentor younger people.
- **Stay independent**: Even in older age, Aries can prefer doing things on their own. They might not like to rely on others unless it is truly necessary.
- **Be protective**: Grandchildren or younger relatives might find that Aries seniors stand up for them with the same fierce loyalty that they showed earlier in life.

While everyone ages in different ways, an Aries often keeps that adventurous spark inside. Health or life changes might slow them down, but their spirit of "Let's try" can remain. The biggest challenge can be adjusting to physical limits and learning to rest when the body needs it.

## 10. Common Lessons for Aries Through Each Life Stage

While Aries is eager to act, there are certain lessons that can appear over and over. If an Aries child, teen, or adult can work on these lessons, they might find it easier to live happily with their inborn fire:

1. **Patience**: Rushing is not always best. Slowing down to plan can prevent mistakes.
2. **Respect for Others**: Not everyone loves quick decisions. Listening helps Aries connect better.
3. **Handling Anger Kindly**: Strong feelings are normal, but Aries should find ways to calm down before reacting.

4. **Staying Flexible**: Life does not always follow the plan. Learning to adapt prevents frustration.
  5. **Appreciating Quiet Times**: Rest is vital for long-term well-being, even if Aries is used to going fast.

## 11. Support Systems for Growing Aries

At any age, having people around who understand Aries' direct style can help. This could be:

- **Family**: Parents, siblings, or relatives who encourage the Aries child or teen to explore their talents in a safe way.
- **Friends**: Individuals who appreciate Aries' honesty and join in their active ideas.
- **Mentors**: Teachers, coaches, or bosses who see Aries' potential and guide them without dampening their spark.
- **Partners**: In close bonds, Aries often does well with someone who can handle their energy but also knows how to stand firm when needed.

By learning from these support systems, Aries can channel their drive into positive efforts rather than frustration.

## 12. Aries Facing Challenges at Different Ages

- **Young Aries**: Might struggle with sharing or waiting.
- **Teen Aries**: Could clash with authority if they feel unrecognized.
- **Young Adult Aries**: Might leap into choices without looking at the long term.
- **Older Aries**: Can feel restless if life becomes too routine.

**Overcoming These Challenges**

- **Communication**: Aries can learn to express frustrations calmly.
- **Goal Setting**: Even if Aries loves spontaneity, setting some goals can keep them on track.
- **Reflection**: Spending a short time each day or week thinking about what went well and what needs work can reduce repeated mistakes.
- **Adaptability**: Aries can remind themselves that changes in life do not mean failure; they can be a new start.

## 13. The Evolving Aries Character

Across the years, an Aries can grow from a small child with a loud laugh and a love for action into a mature adult who still keeps that spark. The child who said "Let me do it!" might become a grown-up who says, "I'll take the lead on that project." The key difference is that, over time, Aries learns how to handle setbacks, how to share space with others, and how to channel big feelings productively.

- **Balance of Fire**: The Aries fire does not have to burn out or cause harm. Through experience and guidance, Aries can learn to keep that flame bright while avoiding needless conflicts.
- **Self-awareness**: Aries who pay attention to their own patterns—like how quickly they get bored or how they react when angry—are better at managing themselves.

## 14. Aries Hobbies and Interests Through the Years

Aries folks might shift hobbies as they grow, but certain themes can remain:

- **Active pursuits**: Hiking, climbing, dance, or sports can show up at any life stage.
- **Fast-paced games**: Video games or board games with quick action might appeal.
- **Exciting travel**: Aries might enjoy short trips to see new places, even in older age (if health allows).
- **Leadership roles**: Whether it is leading a club in high school or running a neighborhood committee as an adult, Aries likes to be at the front of change.

## 15. Aries and Learning New Skills

Learning never stops, and Aries often loves picking up new abilities—especially if they provide a sense of challenge. From childhood to senior years, Aries might:

- **Jump right in**: They begin practicing as soon as they see something interesting, rather than waiting for detailed instructions.
- **Benefit from variety**: If the lesson is repetitive, Aries might quit. But if there is room for creativity or rapid progress, they thrive.
- **Need to pace themselves**: Aries can try to master everything in one go. A step-by-step approach can prevent burnout.

## 16. Handling Big Life Events

Throughout life, Aries might face major crossroads—changing schools, starting a job, moving to a new home, etc. They often see these moments as calls to action. Instead of overthinking, Aries might start planning right away. This direct approach can be helpful but can also lead to overlooked details. Talking to someone who can provide a balanced view is often wise.

- **Example**: If an Aries teen wants to switch schools to pursue a certain subject, they might jump into the process without checking if the new school truly has what they need. A calm chat with a counselor can fill in the missing facts.
- **Another example**: If an Aries adult wants to change jobs, they might quit before securing a new one. Sometimes that works out, but other times they may end up stressed about finances. A bit of planning can ease the risk.

## 17. Aries in Groups and Communities

Aries can be a force for good in a community. They might:

- **Speak up for others**: Aries does not like unfairness. If they see something wrong, they might try to fix it.
- **Organize events**: With their energy, Aries might help gather people for a shared goal (like a neighborhood cleanup or a sports day).
- **Motivate the shy**: By showing confidence, Aries can inspire those who are less sure of themselves.

The main caution is not to overshadow others. Aries should remember to ask for opinions and let quieter people have a turn leading. This approach ensures everyone feels valued.

## 18. Aries and Self-Care Over Time

Because Aries is so active, there can be a risk of burnout or stress. Taking care of mental and physical well-being is essential:

- **Physical self-care**: Rest days, stretching, balanced meals, and plenty of water can keep energy stable.
- **Emotional self-care**: A short time each day to relax, read, draw, or do something soothing can calm Aries' busy mind.

- **Healthy boundaries**: Aries might love to jump into new tasks, but saying "no" sometimes can protect them from overload.

## 19. Watching the Aries Spark Mature

Looking at an Aries child who is loud and adventurous, one might wonder if they will calm down. Some Aries do settle a bit, but the spark usually remains. The difference is that a mature Aries learns how and when to use it. They might still get excited about a new plan or stand up fast if they see wrongdoing, but they also know how to pause, consider next steps, and look at who else is involved.

- **Example of growth**: A young Aries might yell at a friend who accidentally broke their toy. An older Aries might first ask, "Are you okay? It's just a toy—maybe we can fix it together." They still show directness, but with understanding.

# CHAPTER 10: FAMOUS ARIES & THEIR LIVES

Throughout history, many well-known people have been born under the Aries sign. They come from different fields—music, acting, art, invention, politics, sports, and more. While it would be wrong to say that their successes only came from being Aries, we can see certain Aries qualities in their work and stories. In this chapter, we will look at a selection of famous Aries, examining how their boldness, eagerness, or quick decision-making might have appeared in their lives. We will not claim that their astrology sign caused their achievements, but we can note patterns that fit the Aries spirit.

## 1. Artists and Thinkers

**Leonardo da Vinci (Born April 15, 1452)**

Leonardo da Vinci was a painter, inventor, and thinker during the Renaissance. He is known for works like the "Mona Lisa" and "The Last Supper." Some sources list his birthday on April 15, making him an Aries. Da Vinci's endless curiosity and range of talents could match the Aries trait of jumping into many interests. He was not only an artist but also studied anatomy, engineering, and science. This wide exploration suggests a drive similar to an Aries' wish to learn through doing. He often tested new techniques in painting and engineering. This bold spirit led to ideas that were ahead of his time.

- **Aries-like traits**: Eager curiosity, willingness to try new methods, and a direct approach to studying nature.

- **Lasting impression**: Da Vinci's notebooks show sketches of inventions like flying machines, demonstrating an active mind that fits the Aries energy.

### Vincent van Gogh (Born March 30, 1853)

Vincent van Gogh was a painter whose works became famous after his death. Born on March 30, he is often listed as an Aries. Van Gogh had a passionate, intense nature, pouring strong feelings into bright, swirling paintings. Although he faced mental health problems, his letters show a person full of deep emotion, longing for understanding, and willing to experiment with bold colors. Some might connect this passion and risk-taking to the Aries spirit, which can lead a person to keep trying despite struggles.

- **Aries-like traits**: Emotional intensity, brave use of color and style, and a strong drive to paint again and again.
- **Lasting impression**: Van Gogh's style was revolutionary, showing that Aries bravery in breaking away from past standards.

## 2. Music Icons

### Lady Gaga (Born March 28, 1986)

Lady Gaga is known for her strong voice, theatrical performances, and bold fashion choices. She started performing in clubs before finding mainstream success. Her openness and willingness to take creative risks echo the Aries spark. She often changes her image or tries out new styles, refusing to be limited by industry norms. This directness in standing up for herself and for causes she believes in can match Aries' sense of fairness and protection.

- **Aries-like traits**: Bold self-expression, fearless approach to new ideas, and strong drive to lead in her field.

- **Achievements**: Multiple awards in music and acting, along with recognition for her activism.

### Mariah Carey (Born March 27, 1969)

Mariah Carey, with her remarkable vocal range, rose to fame in the early 1990s. Known for hits like "Vision of Love" and "Hero," she has set records on music charts. Her birthday is March 27, placing her in Aries territory. She has shown a persistent, driven side throughout her career, often writing or co-writing her songs and pushing for creative control over her albums. Many have noted her ability to bounce back from setbacks, another trait often linked to the Aries sign.

- **Aries-like traits**: Strong will to shape her own career, quick recovery from professional challenges, and an eye for bold, memorable performances.
- **Lasting impression**: Carey's success, including a high number of chart-topping singles, shows the Aries push to stand out and achieve big goals.

## 3. Actors and Performers

### Robert Downey Jr. (Born April 4, 1965)

Robert Downey Jr. is a well-known actor who played major roles like Tony Stark (Iron Man) in the Marvel films and Sherlock Holmes in modern adaptations. Born on April 4, he has spoken about facing personal struggles earlier in life. Yet, he made a strong comeback, showing resilience, which can be a strong Aries trait: the ability to rise again after falling. Downey's witty, confident style in his roles often reflects an Aries-like charm and directness. Fans admire his openness and the drive he shows to keep improving.

- **Aries-like traits**: Bold personality, resilience, and eagerness to take on challenging roles.
- **Impact**: He became one of Hollywood's highest-paid actors, symbolizing how an Aries can reclaim success even after setbacks.

**Emma Watson (Born April 15, 1990)**

Emma Watson rose to fame playing Hermione Granger in the "Harry Potter" films. Born on April 15, she is an Aries who later balanced acting with studying at a university and taking on advocacy work. Her readiness to speak publicly on causes, such as equality, aligns with Aries' protective streak. She also shows a blend of intelligence and directness, which many associate with Aries. By managing her career while staying active in important issues, she displays both Aries energy and a steady sense of personal direction.

- **Aries-like traits**: Courage in speaking out, taking on new challenges (acting in different types of films, pursuing higher education), and balanced leadership.
- **Lasting effect**: Watson's voice in global matters highlights the Aries drive to protect fairness and champion causes.

## 4. Sports Figures

**Peyton Manning (Born March 24, 1976)**

Peyton Manning is an American football quarterback known for his leadership and skill on the field. Born on March 24, he is often cited as an Aries example in sports. His approach to football involved quick thinking, careful planning, and a commanding presence in the huddle. While quick thinking can align with Aries, he also showed patience and study—traits that might go beyond the common Aries style. Even so, his will to win, direct commands to teammates, and boldness in big games can reflect the Aries desire to lead and achieve.

- **Aries-like traits**: Leadership, strong mental focus, and readiness to take action on the field.
- **Record**: He became one of the most successful quarterbacks in the National Football League (NFL), highlighting a driven nature.

**Ayrton Senna (Born March 21, 1960)**

Ayrton Senna was a famous Formula One racing driver from Brazil. Though different sources list slightly different birth data, many point to March 21 as his birthday, marking him as an Aries at the start of the sign. He was known for his passion and fearless driving style. He took big risks on the track, often pulling off moves that showed quick reflexes and a bold willingness to push limits. This intensity carried both triumphs and dangers.

- **Aries-like traits**: Bravery in high-risk situations, a direct approach to challenges, and a strong urge to compete at the highest level.
- **Legacy**: He remains admired as one of the greatest racing drivers, reflecting how Aries fire can lead to outstanding achievements.

## 5. Political and Social Leaders

Many leaders worldwide are born under Aries, though their success or policies may not always match the warmest aspects of the sign. Still, the Aries traits of direct action, strong will, and a forward-looking view can appear in some political figures. Instead of focusing on controversies, we can note how Aries-like qualities of bold leadership or quick decisions might shape their actions.

## Thomas Jefferson (Born April 13, 1743)

Thomas Jefferson was an American Founding Father and the third President of the United States. He helped write the Declaration of Independence. Born on April 13, he fits the Aries date range. Jefferson was known for wide interests—politics, science, architecture—and for playing a leading role in shaping new ideas for his country. His willingness to stand for certain principles and push for big changes can be linked to Aries' sense of bold action and fresh starts.

- **Aries-like traits**: Drive to make change, independence, and a curious mind that explored many areas.
- **Influence**: As a main author of key documents, Jefferson showed how an Aries can shape new systems.

## 6. Business and Innovation Figures

Though many business leaders do not talk much about zodiac signs, some well-known founders or CEOs happen to be Aries. They might show Aries traits like risk-taking, direct speech, or a strong push to lead.

### Larry Page (Born March 26, 1973)

Larry Page, born on March 26, is one of the co-founders of Google. He helped create the search engine that transformed how people find information. As a leader, Page often pushed for innovative thinking. This can match Aries' love of trying new things and improving old methods. Google's rapid growth and continuous expansion into new areas (like self-driving cars, artificial intelligence, and more) might reflect the Aries drive to keep moving forward without fear of mistakes.

- **Aries-like traits**: Innovation, eagerness to break boundaries, and bold leadership decisions.
- **Outcome**: Google grew into one of the biggest tech companies in the world, showing that a strong push for action can lead to major changes in everyday life.

## 7. Writers and Public Figures

Plenty of Aries have shared their ideas in books or in public roles. Their writing or speaking style can show the Aries directness or passion.

**Maya Angelou (Born April 4, 1928)**

Maya Angelou was an American poet, writer, and civil rights activist. While not everyone agrees on exact birth times for historical reasons, her commonly accepted date is April 4, placing her in Aries. She wrote with strong emotion about life experiences, social issues, and personal growth. Her spoken words carried a powerful tone that inspired many. Her Aries side could be seen in her fearless approach to discussing tough subjects and her drive to uplift people with honest storytelling.

- **Aries-like traits**: Bold expression, willingness to speak about injustice, and a strong sense of personal voice.
- **Impact**: Her writings and talks remain important, proving how an Aries can use direct communication to promote understanding.

## 8. Patterns Among Famous Aries

When we look at these and other Aries figures, a few themes may stand out:

1. **Bravery and Risk-Taking**: Many Aries do not shy away from trying something new or stepping outside normal limits. This can lead to breakthroughs in art, science, sports, or business.
2. **Passionate Expression**: Aries often pour strong emotion into their work, whether it is painting, singing, acting, or writing.
3. **Direct Style**: Aries might speak their mind or approach tasks head-on. This can be an asset when quick action is needed, though it can also cause conflicts if others need a more measured pace.
4. **Resilience**: A number of Aries celebrities and notable people have faced setbacks (financial issues, health challenges, controversies) yet bounced back with renewed drive.
5. **Broad Interests**: Some Aries, like Leonardo da Vinci, branch out into many fields. Their active mind seeks variety. This can result in a diverse legacy.

## 9. Common Misconceptions

It can be easy to assume that all Aries who become famous do so because of "Aries energy." In reality, many factors—talent, resources, hard work, timing—shape success. Astrology alone does not decide a person's future. Also, many people are unaware of their full birth chart, which includes more than just the Sun sign. Still, it can be fun to see how Aries traits appear in those who have reached wide recognition.

- **Not all Aries act the same**: Some Aries are more introverted, some more extroverted. Famous Aries might show strong outer traits, but everyday Aries folks can be quieter.
- **Shared birthdays**: Just because someone shares a birthday with a famous Aries does not mean they will have a similar life path. It is a reminder that signs can point to tendencies, not fixed outcomes.

## 10. Learning from Famous Aries

Whether one believes strongly in astrology or not, we can still draw lessons from how these individuals used courage, directness, and strong will to shape their paths. An Aries child might find inspiration in how someone overcame obstacles, took a chance, or invented a new style. An adult Aries might see how important it is to balance that spark with patience, teamwork, or deeper planning. Some ways to learn from these examples include:

1. **Set Big Goals**: Aries thrives on having something exciting to strive for. Whether it is in art, science, or sports, aiming high can spark creativity.
2. **Keep Going**: If things do not work out at first, remember that many well-known Aries faced failures before they succeeded. Resilience is often key.
3. **Stay True to Your Style**: Many Aries in the public eye are known for a unique approach or for refusing to follow the crowd. This can be a reminder that originality can pay off.
4. **Mind Others' Needs**: While forging ahead, Aries can still remember to consider how their actions affect those around them. Many famous Aries worked with teams or had mentors.

## 11. Missteps and Criticisms

Famous Aries, like anyone, can make mistakes. Some have been called out for rash decisions, strong tempers, or refusing to back down from bad plans. These issues reflect the challenging side of Aries traits. Yet, we can see that those who learn from their errors often grow stronger. For example, Robert Downey Jr. overcame legal troubles and personal problems, emerging as a major star after taking time to change his path.

- **Lesson**: Confidence is good, but ignoring wise advice can lead to trouble. A balanced Aries learns when to pause and reflect.

- **Ongoing growth**: Many Aries personalities show that transformation is possible at any age if one is willing to adapt.

## 12. Different Fields, Same Spark

As shown in our examples, Aries people appear in every walk of life:

- **Art**: Da Vinci and Van Gogh used bold methods, going beyond what others thought normal.
- **Music**: Lady Gaga and Mariah Carey represent strong vocals, stage presence, and a push for uniqueness.
- **Acting**: Robert Downey Jr. and Emma Watson highlight resilience and direct advocacy.
- **Sports**: Peyton Manning's leadership and Ayrton Senna's fearless racing both show Aries willingness to face challenges.
- **Innovation**: Larry Page's approach at Google matched Aries' restlessness for new possibilities.

We see the Aries traits playing out in different ways, but the common thread is taking action, going beyond limits, and having a certain boldness in approaching work.

## 13. Global Aries Figures

Aries people are found worldwide, so the examples above barely scratch the surface. Every country has leaders, artists, or innovators born under Aries. These individuals often make a mark by refusing to stay with the status quo, pushing for change, or expressing themselves in direct ways. They can be beloved or controversial, but seldom ignored.

- **Cultural variations**: Different cultures view boldness and directness in various ways. An Aries in one culture might be praised for initiative, while in another, they might be told to slow down.

- **Modern and historical**: From ancient rulers to modern activists, Aries individuals span all periods. Their sign is always linked to the same themes: action, leadership, and dynamic energy.

## 14. How Aries Traits Can Appear Differently

Even within the Aries sign, personalities vary. Some Aries show their spark through quiet determination rather than loud expressions. Others might channel their energy into planning rather than outward action. A famous Aries who is known for painting might handle challenges differently than a famous Aries who is known for politics. The sign alone does not dictate the path, but it can color the way they pursue goals.

## 15. Aries as Role Models

It can help young Aries (or people of any sign) to see stories of well-known Aries who overcame odds. If a child or teen looks up to an Aries musician, for example, they might learn the value of practicing daily or standing firm in their artistic choices. If they admire an Aries athlete, they might pick up tips on discipline, physical fitness, or mental focus. Of course, picking role models should include a look at their character as well, because not all famous people set a good example in every part of life.

## 16. Media Portrayals of Aries

Sometimes, shows or articles highlight a celebrity's sign. This can be fun but might also be oversimplified. A headline might say, "This star is such an Aries!" when they do something bold, ignoring the fact that real personalities are complex. Still, for those who enjoy astrology, it can be neat to spot patterns or discuss how a sign's traits might show up in the celebrity's behavior.

## 17. Aries and Awards

Many Aries have received top awards in their fields—Oscars, Grammys, sports trophies, or scientific honors. Their willingness to fight for a high standard can result in shining moments. Yet not all Aries chase awards. Some prefer personal satisfaction, pushing forward simply because they love what they do. Recognition can be a byproduct of that unstoppable Aries will.

## 18. Inspiring Confidence

One of the biggest lessons from famous Aries is to believe in oneself enough to try. Even if they faced rejection or doubt, these individuals took a chance on their ideas or talents. For someone who feels unsure, reading about an Aries who kept going can spark courage. It reminds us that success stories often include struggles behind the scenes.

## 19. Learning from Downfalls

Famous Aries who had big downfalls—be it financial trouble, canceled projects, or public criticism—also show that a bold approach can lead to risky choices. When Aries energy is not channeled wisely, one might jump too fast or ignore warnings. However, the ability to recover is also part of many Aries stories. Failing does not have to be the end; it can be the start of a new plan.

# CHAPTER 11: HANDLING EMOTIONS AS AN ARIES

Emotions can be strong for many Aries folks. Because this sign is linked to fire, people often say Aries has intense feelings that spark up fast, whether that feeling is joy, anger, excitement, or disappointment. While having strong emotions can bring passion and energy, it can also lead to challenges if those emotions become too overwhelming or if they hurt relationships. In this chapter, we will explore how Aries might handle different feelings, what triggers certain emotional reactions, and how an Aries person can find healthy ways to express themselves. This chapter aims to give ideas that Aries people can use in their daily lives so that their bright flame of emotion remains helpful and not destructive.

## 1. The Nature of Aries Emotions

Aries people often experience their emotions in a bold and open way. They might not keep their feelings hidden for long because they typically do not like to pretend. If an Aries is happy, they might laugh out loud and appear more energetic than usual. If they feel upset, they might show that, too—sometimes quickly. This direct, unhidden style can be refreshing because it leaves little room for guessing. However, it can also lead to misunderstandings if others are not prepared for Aries' strong responses.

- **Positives of open emotion**: Others know where they stand with Aries. There are fewer secrets, and problems can be addressed before they grow bigger.
- **Potential downsides**: If emotions boil over too fast, Aries might say or do something they regret. Others may see Aries

as too dramatic or quick-tempered if the reactions are not managed well.

## 2. Common Emotional Triggers for Aries

Every person has certain issues that might spark frustration, sadness, or enthusiasm. For Aries, some common triggers include:

1. **Feeling of Unfairness**: Aries tends to speak out if they see someone picking on a friend or bending the rules. That sense of defending what is right can lead to an instant emotional surge.
2. **Blocked Plans**: Aries loves moving forward. If they have a plan and it is blocked by red tape, slow decision-making, or unexpected obstacles, they might feel deeply annoyed.
3. **Waiting in Lines or Delays**: Patience can be a challenge for Aries, so a long wait or a delay can spark impatience, which might turn into anger if not managed.
4. **Lack of Freedom**: Aries values independence. If someone tries to control their actions without good reason, Aries might respond with resistance or frustration.
5. **Sudden Changes in Loved Ones**: If a close friend or partner pulls away suddenly, Aries might feel both anger and sadness. Aries often needs direct talk, so mysterious behavior can set off strong emotions.

By understanding what tends to cause emotional surges, Aries can prepare ahead of time. It is easier to plan coping methods when you know what situations are likely to upset you.

## 3. Anger and Impulsiveness

One of the most noted Aries emotions is anger that appears quickly. Because Aries is linked to action and fire, the sign can get heated when something goes wrong. This anger might show up in various ways:

- **Short outbursts**: Aries might snap or shout, then calm down after a brief storm.
- **Physical restlessness**: They might pace around, tap their foot, or need to do something active to blow off steam.
- **Direct confrontation**: An Aries might want to address the problem head-on, whether it is with a friend, family member, or stranger.

While short anger can sometimes solve a small problem (clearing the air right away), too much anger can harm relationships or cause regretful actions. For this reason, Aries often benefits from anger-management strategies that let them release tension in a safer way.

## 4. Strategies for Calming Down Quickly

Because Aries might not enjoy staying angry for long, it helps to have simple methods to calm down before saying or doing something hurtful. Some Aries-friendly methods include:

1. **Physical Break**: Go for a short walk, do a quick set of exercises, or practice breathing deeply. Physical activity can help release built-up tension.
2. **Count to Ten**: This classic tip gives a small pause before speaking. Even a ten-second gap can help Aries spot if they are about to say something they do not really mean.
3. **Use "I" Statements**: Instead of shouting, "You're making me mad!" Aries can say, "I feel upset because I thought we agreed

on something else." This keeps the focus on feelings rather than blame.
4. **Leave the Room**: If anger is too hot, stepping away for a short time can cool the emotions. Aries might say, "I need a few minutes to calm down," and return when they feel more balanced.

Practicing these calm-down methods can be tough for Aries at first because they prefer quick action. However, repeating them over time can become second nature, helping them avoid regrets.

## 5. Handling Sadness or Disappointment

People often link Aries with anger or excitement, but sadness is also part of life. Aries might feel disappointed if a big plan falls through, or if someone they trust lets them down. Unlike some signs that withdraw and stay quiet when sad, Aries might react with frustration or impulsiveness even when their core feeling is sadness.

- **Recognizing sadness**: Aries can ask themselves if they are angry or if they are actually hurt. This helps in picking the right method to feel better.
- **Ways to cope**: Some Aries find it helpful to talk with a good friend or take part in a physical or creative activity to release emotions. For instance, painting, writing, or playing a musical instrument can give an outlet for feelings.

It is important for Aries to understand that sadness is not a sign of weakness. Admitting disappointment or grief can be a step to healing. Once Aries faces the sadness, they can take action to address what caused it, whether that means finding a new goal, seeking comfort, or talking to someone they trust.

## 6. Excitement and Joy

Aries is known for a bright spirit when things are going well. This excitement can be contagious, inspiring friends and family to join in the fun. Aries might shout with joy, jump around, or flash a big grin. They might also make quick plans—"Let's go somewhere right now!"—because they want to share the positive energy.

- **Upside**: This sense of joy can bring people together. Aries can lift the mood of a room with their enthusiasm.
- **Caution**: If Aries goes overboard, they might take risks that are not thought out. It is still wise to keep some balance, even in happy times.

Expressing joy helps Aries release stress and bond with loved ones. Some might channel excitement into creative hobbies or group activities. The key is to remember not everyone has the same energy level. By letting others move at their own pace, Aries can avoid feeling let down if no one is quite as excited as they are.

## 7. Dealing with Fear or Worry

Aries is often seen as brave, yet everyone feels fear sometimes. An Aries might worry about failing, losing someone they care about, or not meeting their own high expectations. Because pride can be strong for Aries, they might hide these worries behind a confident front. Over time, hidden worries can grow bigger.

- **Recognizing worry**: If an Aries finds themselves restless at night, frequently annoyed over small things, or avoiding certain tasks, it might be a sign of underlying fear.
- **Facing it**: Talking to a trusted friend or professional can help. Aries does not have to handle fear alone. Writing fears down might also help clarify them and suggest possible solutions.

Worry can often be reduced by taking small steps. For instance, if Aries worries about a test at school or a project at work, studying or preparing steadily can shrink that fear. Aries loves action, so turning worry into purposeful steps can be a powerful tool.

## 8. Emotional Expression in Relationships

In close relationships, Aries might show love with warmth and direct action. However, emotional misunderstandings can happen if the other person needs a calmer approach. Aries might appear too intense or, at times, too blunt. Here are some ways Aries can share feelings in a balanced way:

1. **Ask Questions**: Instead of just stating, "This is how I feel," Aries can ask, "How do you feel about this?" This invites two-way communication.
2. **Active Listening**: Aries can practice focusing on the loved one's words before responding. They can repeat back what they heard to ensure they understand.
3. **Gentle Words**: Even when emotions run high, using a calm tone can keep the discussion open. Aries might learn to say, "I feel upset, but I value your view. Let's discuss carefully," instead of snapping.

When Aries invests energy in hearing loved ones out, it can prevent small emotional bumps from turning into bigger conflicts. Aries' directness can be a strength, as long as it is paired with patience and respect.

## 9. Balancing Individual Feelings and Group Harmony

Aries can sometimes clash with group needs if their emotions push them to act right away. In a group project or family matter, Aries might jump to a solution that feels right to them without fully checking if everyone is on board. This can cause emotional friction.

- **Key approach**: Recognize that a group can have many feelings. Aries can help by saying, "Here's my idea, but let's hear all thoughts before deciding."
- **Look for signals**: If other group members seem uneasy, Aries can pause and ask what is bothering them. This step can prevent bigger emotional blowups later.

By balancing personal drive with group harmony, Aries can become a trusted team player. This not only helps the group succeed but also reduces tension that might lead to emotional burnout.

## 10. Long-Term Emotional Growth

Aries might start life with quick bursts of emotion, both positive and negative. Over time, learning from each situation is key to growth. For instance, an Aries who once yelled during every conflict might learn to pause, speak calmly, and solve problems faster. A few steps that help in this long-term process include:

1. **Reflection**: Setting aside a short time each week to think about emotional highs and lows can reveal patterns. Aries can ask, "What triggered my big emotions this week? How did I handle them?"
2. **Goal Setting**: Aries might set an emotional goal—"I will practice staying calm when plans fall through," or "I will focus on speaking kindly even if I'm upset."
3. **Reward Progress**: When an Aries sees improvement in handling tough feelings, they can give themselves a small reward. This is not bragging; it is reinforcing good habits.
4. **Seek Support**: Whether it is a friend, counselor, or family member, having someone to talk to helps Aries keep track of emotional progress.

Over months and years, these efforts can lead to a calmer, steadier emotional life without losing that bright Aries spark.

# 11. Healthy Outlets for Aries Feelings

Because Aries is active, physical and creative outlets can serve as healthy ways to manage emotions. Some examples:

- **Exercise**: Activities like running, martial arts, dancing, or even a quick home workout can channel anger, stress, or restless excitement into movement.
- **Artistic Pursuits**: Drawing, painting, writing poems, or composing music can help Aries translate emotions into a tangible form.
- **Volunteering**: Helping in community tasks might let Aries use their energy for a good cause, which can lift their mood and give a sense of purpose.
- **Hobbies with Elements of Challenge**: Aries might enjoy puzzle-solving games, building projects, or interactive tasks that keep the mind and body engaged.

These pursuits give Aries a place to put extra emotion. They also provide a sense of achievement, which can soothe frustration and boost a stable mood.

# 12. The Role of Communication

Emotions are not only personal; they often affect others. Good communication helps Aries share feelings in a way that fosters connection rather than conflict. Some communication tips include:

1. **Choose Timing**: If Aries is upset, it might help to wait until they are calmer to approach someone about the issue. Otherwise, words could be harsher than intended.
2. **Focus on Facts**: When discussing a problem, Aries can point out the facts ("When this happened, I felt left out") rather than labeling the other person ("You always ignore me!").

3. **Listen to Solutions**: Aries might have a ready solution in mind, but the other person could have a different fix. Hearing all ideas can stop the conflict from escalating.

Clear, kind communication can show Aries' passion while respecting others' perspectives. This approach prevents misunderstandings that can spark unnecessary emotions.

## 13. Learning to Apologize and Forgive

Because Aries can react quickly, they might say or do something in anger and regret it later. Apologizing does not come easily to everyone, but it is a crucial skill for building healthy emotional ties. An effective apology from an Aries can look like this:

- **Admit the Action**: "I'm sorry I shouted at you."
- **Acknowledge the Effect**: "I see that it hurt your feelings and made you upset."
- **Say How You Will Improve**: "Next time, I'll try to calm down before talking."

Similarly, forgiving others is also important. Aries might hold onto frustration if they feel someone betrayed them. Learning to let go can free Aries from carrying anger around. Forgiveness does not mean forgetting or approving of what happened; it means accepting that it is over and choosing not to hold onto resentment.

## 14. Overcoming Emotional Roadblocks

Sometimes an Aries might face a deeper emotional challenge, such as heartbreak, grief, or a major disappointment that does not fade quickly. In such times, the usual quick methods of relief might not be enough. Here are steps Aries can consider:

1. **Allow Emotions**: Instead of forcing themselves to "get over it," Aries can give themselves time to feel sad, confused, or frustrated. This does not imply weakness.
2. **Seek Guidance**: A counselor, mentor, or support group can offer tools for navigating deeper emotional wounds. Aries does not have to solve everything alone.
3. **Focus on Self-Care**: Activities like resting properly, eating balanced meals, and maintaining a regular exercise schedule can keep Aries physically strong while they heal emotionally.
4. **Gradual Goals**: Aries might pick small steps, like reintroducing a hobby or connecting with supportive friends, to slowly rebuild confidence and happiness.

While Aries likes fast solutions, deep emotional wounds often heal over time. Patience and compassion for oneself are vital in such situations.

## 15. Aries and Emotional Honesty

One strength of Aries is the ability to be honest about emotions. They might say, "I feel angry right now," or "I'm so excited I can't sit still." This honesty can help others trust an Aries person. But emotional honesty also involves being truthful about harder feelings, like anxiety or sadness. Aries might feel that admitting such feelings shows weakness, but in reality, it shows courage to be open about vulnerability.

- **Benefits**: Openness builds deeper connections with friends, family, and partners. People understand Aries better when they know what is really happening inside.
- **Caution**: Sharing every single thought the moment it appears might overwhelm others. Aries can learn to filter and pick the right time to express bigger feelings.

## 16. Self-Talk and Mood

Aries might talk to themselves in a strong, direct way, which can impact mood. If the self-talk is negative ("I messed up everything again!"), Aries could become angry or lose confidence. Positive self-talk can flip this around: "I made a mistake, but I can fix it by doing X, Y, and Z." Because Aries tends to act on what they think, controlling that inner voice can shape how they handle emotions each day.

- **Ideas to improve self-talk**:
    - Replace negative statements with problem-solving phrases.
    - Notice small wins each day, even if they seem minor.
    - Practice praising yourself for showing patience or kindness.

## 17. Observing Patterns and Making Changes

Because Aries is forward-moving, they might not spend much time reviewing old patterns. Yet noticing patterns can help them avoid repeating emotional mistakes. For instance, if an Aries sees that they always lose their temper before lunchtime, maybe they need a snack or a quick break. If they notice they are most restless on Monday mornings, maybe they can schedule a fun activity or a short run on Sunday night to prepare.

- **Keeping a log**: A simple journal of emotional ups and downs, along with what was happening at the time, can reveal triggers. Once a pattern is spotted, Aries can try small adjustments—like shifting schedules or changing routines—to lessen emotional stress.

## 18. Aries and Group Support

There may be times when an Aries benefits from talking with others who have had similar emotional experiences. Group discussions or forums—where people share how they handle quick anger, impatience, or over-the-top excitement—can provide useful tips. Aries can also share their own successes, which can be motivating to the rest of the group. This sense of shared struggle can remind Aries they are not alone in dealing with big feelings.

- **Examples**: Local anger management classes, online forums for coping strategies, or support circles for those going through a tough time.
- **Outcome**: Learning from others can speed up emotional growth because Aries sees fresh ideas and tries them out right away.

## 19. Celebrating Emotional Wins

Emotional growth does not happen overnight. When an Aries handles a tough emotional situation well, it can help to mark the achievement in a positive way. Maybe they kept calm in an argument for the first time, or they spoke up about sadness instead of hiding it. Recognizing these wins can boost Aries' confidence and inspire them to keep building healthier habits.

- **Ways to mark emotional wins**:
    1. Write it in a journal: "Today, I stayed calm in a heated talk at work."
    2. Tell a friend: "Hey, I used to get upset quickly, but this time I stayed level-headed."
    3. Reward with self-care: Take a relaxing bath, watch a favorite show, or do something else that feels gentle and comforting.

By noting these improvements, Aries can see real progress and remain motivated to handle emotions wisely.

## 20. Putting It All Together

Emotions are a core part of life for everyone, but Aries experiences them with a certain fire and directness that can be powerful when channeled well. From quick anger to deep excitement, Aries often wears the heart on the sleeve. While this can bring moments of friction, it also creates a life filled with passion and honesty. By learning to pause, listen, and direct emotions into positive outlets, Aries can build relationships that flourish, handle work or school challenges with more ease, and remain true to the fiery spirit that makes this sign so unique.

In the end, being an Aries with strong emotions is not about shutting down the flame; it is about learning to guide it. Whether through quick calming methods, supportive conversations, regular reflection, or healthy outlets, Aries people can keep their emotional energy bright and helpful. With patience, practice, and honest self-awareness, they can turn raw feelings into a powerful resource that fuels both personal growth and connection with others.

# CHAPTER 12: ARIES & WORK LIFE

Work is a major part of adult life, and Aries often approaches it with a strong sense of drive and eagerness. Whether the Aries person is a part-time employee, an entrepreneur, a manager, or a freelancer, certain common traits tend to show up in how they handle tasks, lead teams, and respond to challenges. In this chapter, we will look at Aries in the professional world. We will explore their natural strengths, the pitfalls they might face, and strategies to ensure that Aries' fiery energy leads to success and not burnout. We will also cover how Aries can get along with various coworkers, handle deadlines, and balance ambition with patience.

## 1. Aries at the Start of a Workday

Aries often likes to begin the day with energy. They might walk into the workplace ready to tackle what is ahead. This sense of eagerness can rub off on coworkers who appreciate having someone around with a "let's get moving" attitude. However, Aries can also become irritated if they arrive with big plans and face immediate delays or disorganized workplaces. They might think, "Why isn't everyone ready to go?"

- **Tip**: Aries can use a short morning routine—like reviewing the top goals for the day—to stay focused. This harnesses that initial spark rather than letting it turn into frustration if others are slow to start.

## 2. Career Paths That Suit Aries

Aries can do well in many fields, but some areas may be extra appealing because they match the sign's active style. These can include:

1. **Entrepreneurship**: Aries might enjoy starting their own business because it gives them freedom and a sense of leadership.
2. **Sales and Marketing**: Persuading people, chasing leads, and responding to fast-paced changes can excite Aries.
3. **Event Planning or Project Coordination**: They can handle many moving parts and keep things on schedule, especially if the tasks are short and dynamic.
4. **Emergency Response or Protective Roles**: Jobs like firefighting, rescue work, or security can benefit from Aries' quick action and courage.
5. **Sports, Coaching, or Fitness**: Physical energy, leadership, and a love for challenges can shine here.
6. **Creative Fields**: Some Aries are drawn to design, filmmaking, or other arts that let them express fresh ideas rapidly.

Of course, Aries folks can succeed in nearly any career if they find ways to tap into their energy. The key is seeking roles that allow some level of independence, motion, or direct action.

## 3. Strengths Aries Brings to Work

1. **Enthusiasm**: Aries can light a spark in the workplace. Their excitement for a new project or product can motivate others.
2. **Fast Decision-Making**: When quick calls must be made, Aries does not hesitate. This can be a huge plus in fields where timing is important.
3. **Readiness to Lead**: Aries often takes charge if no one else does. This can keep a team from getting stuck in indecision.

4. **Goal-Driven**: Aries likes to set targets and work toward them, which can keep a team on track.

When used wisely, these strengths can make an Aries employee or boss a valuable asset to any organization. They are often the ones who push projects forward and refuse to let the group remain idle.

## 4. Possible Work Challenges for Aries

1. **Impatience with Delays**: If the job involves waiting on approvals or dealing with slow processes, Aries might lose motivation or get frustrated.
2. **Short Attention on Details**: Aries may rush tasks that feel boring or repetitive, risking mistakes.
3. **Conflict with Coworkers**: Directness can lead to friction if Aries does not phrase criticism gently.
4. **Burnout**: Putting too much energy in for long periods without rest can exhaust Aries.

Acknowledging these challenges early can help Aries plan strategies to handle them. For instance, if a job has many slow steps, Aries might break it down into smaller goals to keep that sense of progress going.

## 5. Aries and Leadership Roles

Aries tends to be comfortable at the front of a team. They can inspire others with bold ideas and a fearless approach. However, leading well requires more than just excitement. Aries leaders might need to remember that not everyone works at the same pace or with the same style.

- **Good Aries leadership traits**:
    - They encourage quick action.

- They give clear directions.
- They do not shy away from tough calls.
- **Pitfalls for Aries leaders:**

  - They might push people too hard without noticing signs of stress.
  - They might forget to gather input from quieter team members.

Balancing these areas can make Aries a leader who is both dynamic and caring, which tends to earn lasting respect rather than short-term obedience.

## 6. Working Under an Aries Boss

If you have an Aries boss, you might see someone who is direct, expects fast results, and loves fresh ideas. This can be exciting because an Aries boss could reward initiative or creativity. At the same time, they might have little patience for excuses or delays. They might say things like, "We need to fix this now," and get irritated if the fix is not immediate.

- **Success tips for employees:**
  - Show that you are proactive. Aries bosses value employees who do not wait around.
  - Offer solutions, not just problems.
  - Respect the boss's sense of urgency while reminding them gently of any real limits or constraints so that tasks remain achievable.

## 7. Aries as a Teammate

When Aries is part of a group project but not the leader, they can still bring energy and keep the group from stalling. They might volunteer for tasks that call for quick thinking or direct contact with clients. However, they might not be as thrilled about tasks that feel slow or detail-heavy, such as extensive record-keeping.

- **Teamwork tips**:
    - If Aries is paired with someone who is thorough and patient, the team can be balanced. Aries can handle front-end action while the other person manages details.
    - Good communication is key. If Aries tries to run ahead without aligning with the team, confusion arises.

## 8. Dealing with Stress and Deadlines

Aries often faces stress when there are big projects, short deadlines, or unexpected changes. While Aries can thrive under pressure, too much can wear them out. Some ways to handle stress at work include:

1. **Breaks for Physical Movement**: A quick walk or even stretching at a desk can help Aries blow off steam and come back with a clear head.
2. **Set Mini-Goals**: If a deadline is far off, Aries might lose interest. Breaking it into weekly or daily goals keeps the momentum going.
3. **Ask for Help**: Aries might try to shoulder everything alone. Reaching out to a coworker or friend when stuck can ease stress and create teamwork.

By spotting stress signs early—like irritability or trouble focusing—Aries can act before stress builds too high.

## 9. Communication Style at Work

Aries communicates in a direct, sometimes blunt way. In the workplace, this can be good for clarity but might rub sensitive coworkers the wrong way. If Aries says, "This plan is not good," others might feel hurt unless Aries explains kindly what they mean. Some communication tips:

- **Say what is good first**: "I like how you did X, but let's adjust Y."
- **Use constructive language**: Instead of "That's a terrible idea," Aries can say, "I see a problem with that approach. What if we try this?"
- **Listen**: Aries can improve professional ties by giving others time to speak and truly hearing them out. Quick interruptions can damage the flow of ideas.

## 10. Boosting Morale

Because Aries radiates energy, they can lift the team's spirit if they channel it positively. For example, Aries might:

- **Cheer on teammates**: "We got this! Let's keep pushing."
- **Suggest group fun**: A short break to share jokes, or a brief chat about good news before diving back into work.
- **Acknowledge success**: Aries might point out when someone meets a milestone, keeping the environment hopeful.

However, Aries should watch that they do not overshadow others by always being the loudest voice. Encouraging everyone to speak up fosters a sense of unity.

## 11. Handling Workplace Conflicts

Conflicts happen in most workplaces. Aries might be quick to jump in if they see a coworker being treated unfairly. This can be good because it stops problems from festering. But if Aries is personally involved, their anger can flare. Steps Aries can take:

1. **Cool Down First**: If a conflict arises, a short pause can prevent saying something too harsh.
2. **Seek Solutions, Not Just Blame**: Aries can direct the conversation toward "How do we fix this?"
3. **Use a Mediator if Needed**: In big conflicts, a manager or HR person can help guide the talk. Aries should not see this as weakness; it is often how companies maintain fairness.

Quick conflict resolution can keep Aries from staying upset and can preserve professional ties.

## 12. Career Advancement for Aries

Moving up in a career often involves new roles, bigger responsibilities, or leading more people. Aries might actively seek promotions or fresh challenges because they do not enjoy feeling stuck. To advance effectively:

- **Build a Track Record**: Aries can keep a record of successes, like finishing projects early or boosting sales. This shows tangible proof of their value.
- **Network Wisely**: Meeting people across different teams or industries can open doors. Aries' direct style can be refreshing if they also show genuine interest in others' work.
- **Work on Soft Skills**: Communication, empathy, and patience with slower processes are often needed at higher levels. Aries who master these will stand out as well-rounded leaders.

Balancing ambition with respect for the structure of an organization helps Aries move forward without causing friction.

## 13. Changing Jobs or Careers

Aries might grow restless if they feel they have mastered a job and there is no new frontier to tackle. This can lead to a switch in roles, departments, or even entire career fields. While some see frequent job changes as unstable, Aries might view it as part of growth. To ensure wise choices:

1. **Reflect on the Real Reason**: Is it just boredom, or is the role truly limiting?
2. **Plan Before Leaping**: Aries should make sure they have a path forward—maybe a new opportunity lined up, or savings if they are taking a risk.
3. **Exit Gracefully**: Maintaining good relationships at an old job can help Aries in the future, in case references or connections are needed.

Moving on can be a positive step if done with some foresight, matching Aries' need for fresh challenges while minimizing risk.

## 14. Entrepreneurship and Aries

Running one's own business can suit Aries. They get to be their own boss, set the pace, and handle exciting decisions. However, successful entrepreneurship also involves:

- **Detail Work**: Invoices, taxes, planning—these are necessary tasks. Aries might hire someone or use tools to help with these if they find them tedious.
- **Patience with Growth**: Aries might want instant success, but many ventures grow slowly. Building a customer base, refining products, and learning from mistakes takes time.
- **Managing Team Members**: If the business grows, Aries may have employees. That means balancing a leadership role with an open door for feedback.

With determination and a willingness to learn, Aries can thrive as an entrepreneur, turning their spark into a real product or service.

## 15. Work-Life Balance

Aries can become so focused on tasks that they forget to rest or enjoy downtime. Overcommitting might lead to exhaustion or even health issues. Work-life balance is crucial:

1. **Set Boundaries**: Aries might need to decide on cut-off times for checking work messages.
2. **Schedule Breaks**: Planning short getaways or weekend activities can prevent burnout. Aries might see these breaks as tasks for mental health.
3. **Reward Effort**: After completing a big project, it helps to rest briefly before starting the next one. This does not slow Aries down; it helps them stay strong for the long run.

When Aries finds a good balance, they can maintain high energy without crashing.

## 16. Aries and Remote Work

Remote or freelance work has become more common. Aries might enjoy the freedom of working from anywhere, but they must be careful about distractions or isolation. Some tips:

- **Create Structure**: Set clear start and end times, plus planned breaks. Aries thrives with some routine to channel their energy.
- **Stay Connected**: Regular video calls or team chats keep Aries linked to the group, providing the social spark they often crave.
- **Vary Tasks**: If possible, Aries can rotate between different types of tasks throughout the day to avoid boredom.

By mixing freedom with discipline, Aries can flourish in remote settings, tapping into their independence and desire for quick progress.

## 17. Mentoring and Growth

Aries may reach a stage where they can mentor newcomers. This can be a chance to pass on skills while refining leadership qualities. Aries can:

- **Teach by Example**: Show how to tackle tasks quickly, but also explain the reasoning so the mentee learns the full process.
- **Encourage Bravery**: Aries can inspire a trainee to try new methods, reminding them that mistakes are part of growth.
- **Stay Patient**: Mentees might take time to learn. Aries should resist rushing or scolding them, focusing instead on gentle guidance.

In guiding others, Aries also learns to slow down and check that each step is clear. This benefits both the trainee and the Aries mentor.

## 18. Handling Emotional Moments at Work

Emotions can run high in a workplace, and Aries is known for strong reactions. If something goes wrong—a missed deadline, a client complaint—Aries might feel angry or pressured. Chapter 11 covered handling emotions more generally, but at work, Aries should remember to keep things professional:

- **Take a Breather**: If Aries is about to snap, they can step outside or move to a quiet spot for a minute.
- **Use Polite Language**: Even in heated times, Aries can say, "I'm concerned about this issue" instead of "I'm furious with you!"

- **Focus on Solutions**: Aries likes to act, so channel that into fixes: "Let's figure out how to solve this right now."

Keeping emotional balance preserves relationships and shows maturity.

## 19. Recognition and Rewards

Aries appreciates seeing the results of their efforts. They might love receiving awards, public praise, or a simple "good job" from the boss. If an Aries does not feel recognized, they can lose motivation or look for a new workplace that values them. Similarly, Aries leaders should remember to give credit to their teams so they do not come across as taking all the glory.

- **Self-Recognition**: Aries can also track their own progress. For instance, keeping a list of achievements each month can boost confidence, especially when external praise is lacking.
- **Recognizing Others**: Offering a few words of appreciation to coworkers can create a supportive environment. A strong team helps Aries excel, too.

## 20. Building a Fulfilling Career as an Aries

A satisfying work life for Aries likely includes variety, chances for growth, and room to take initiative. Aries can stay motivated by exploring roles that challenge them, stepping up to lead when possible, and seeking excitement in each stage of their career. They also need to remember the importance of cooperation, patience, and emotional control to avoid burning bridges or burning out. By taking advantage of their natural boldness—and balancing it with thoughtful planning—Aries can shape a career that feels both successful and true to their fiery nature.

# CHAPTER 13: ARIES IN DIFFERENT CULTURES

When people hear the word "Aries," they often think of Western astrology with its twelve signs, each linked to particular dates and traits. However, the concept of a ram or a fiery, bold sign appears in many places throughout the world, though not always under the same name. Different societies have created stories, star maps, and customs that may connect to the same group of stars or to an animal like a ram. In this chapter, we will look at how Aries—or ideas similar to Aries—have appeared or been recognized across different cultures. We will also see how various beliefs and systems have described the traits or energies often linked to Aries in the West. The goal is to give a broader view of how the ram sign, or something close to it, has taken shape in different communities.

## 1. Aries in Western Astrology: A Brief Recap

Before exploring other cultures, it helps to do a quick reminder of Aries in Western astrology. Aries is seen as the first sign of the zodiac, covering approximately March 21 to April 19. It is symbolized by the ram, linked to the element of fire, and often described with words like "bold," "active," and "direct." Many Western horoscopes say Aries folks may be driven, quick to start things, and eager to stand up for themselves.

One important note: Western astrology largely stems from Babylonian, Egyptian, and Greek influences that merged over centuries. Ancient cultures in the Mediterranean region looked up at the same group of stars (now called the constellation Aries) and came up with their own stories. Eventually, these ideas blended into what many people in Europe and North America follow today as Western astrology.

## 2. Babylonian and Mesopotamian Roots

Much of Western astrology has its roots in Mesopotamia, an ancient region that covered parts of modern-day Iraq, Kuwait, and Syria. The Babylonians were skillful sky watchers and created one of the earliest forms of astrology that placed the sky into twelve sectors. One of those sectors later became identified with the Ram.

- **Name and Identity**: It is believed the Babylonians connected the stars in what we call Aries with a farmhand, a hired worker, or sometimes a ram-like figure. The exact naming differed over time.
- **Seasonal Link**: In Mesopotamia, the appearance of certain stars helped people guess when floods might happen or when to plant crops. The group of stars for Aries arrived near the start of spring, which was vital for farming.
- **Lasting Impact**: As Greek and later Roman scholars learned from Babylonian star lore, they kept the link between that star cluster and a ram, eventually calling it Aries in Latin.

## 3. Ancient Egypt and the Ram-Headed Gods

In Egypt, people had their own sky stories, but rams also played a role in some of their religious images. For example, a few Egyptian gods were shown with ram heads or horns. One well-known figure was Khnum, an older deity often depicted with a ram's head. Though this does not match exactly with the Greek notion of the constellation Aries, the shared image of a ram is notable.

- **Khnum's Role**: Khnum was linked to the source of the Nile River and was thought to help form humans on a potter's wheel. He symbolized creation and fresh beginnings, which

interestingly lines up with Aries' place at the start of the zodiac cycle.
- **Star Observations**: Egyptian priests and astronomers also tracked the skies. While they had different names for the constellations, they recognized that certain star groups lined up with times of the year. The group we call Aries likely fell under their watchful eye, but it was not always singled out as a separate constellation in the same way the Greeks did.

Though Egyptian culture did not form an "Aries" sign in the modern sense, the importance of ram symbols for power, new life, and protection can be seen as loosely parallel to Aries themes in Western astrology.

## 4. Aries-Like Ideas in Greek and Roman Lore

We have covered Greek and Roman stories in earlier chapters. The golden ram story, with Phrixus and Helle, is a key myth linked to Aries in Western tradition. In Roman times, the name Aries (Latin for "ram") stuck. Mars, the Roman god of war, became the ruler of Aries in astrology. This war god link highlights bravery, action, and daring, which are all Aries traits in modern horoscopes.

The Romans spread many Greek-based myths across their empire, so the Aries concept traveled widely. This is how Aries eventually took root in much of Europe and, by extension, influenced later Western astrology in places such as the Americas.

## 5. The Ram Symbol Beyond Europe

Rams appear as important animals in many other cultures worldwide, even if those cultures did not call the same star group "Aries." People have long respected the ram's strength, horns, and protective nature. This can echo Aries-like traits of courage, boldness, and forward drive.

- **Middle Eastern Traditions**: In some Middle Eastern lands, rams have been symbols of sacrifice, leadership, or guardianship. Though these ideas do not directly match "Aries" as a zodiac sign, they show that the ram stands for power and bravery in many places.
- **African Beliefs**: Various groups in Africa have stories about sheep or rams that might bring luck or hold spiritual meaning. While these tales might not link the animal to a star sign, they still show admiration for its qualities.
- **Asian Countries**: Although many Asian cultures follow different systems (for example, the Chinese zodiac), the concept of a horned animal as strong or vital is not rare. However, it is often represented by goats, sheep, or other horned creatures, rather than exactly the Western "ram."

## 6. Chinese Zodiac: Where Is the Ram?

The Chinese zodiac is very different from the Western system. Instead of dividing the year into twelve parts, the Chinese zodiac assigns an animal to each year in a 12-year cycle. The animals include the Rat, Ox, Tiger, Rabbit, Dragon, Snake, Horse, Goat (or Sheep), Monkey, Rooster, Dog, and Pig.

- **Goat/Sheep vs. Ram**: Some people wonder if the Goat or Sheep in the Chinese zodiac is similar to Aries. While a goat or sheep can have horns, the Chinese zodiac's Goat/Sheep year covers a full year rather than a segment like March to April. People born in that year share certain traits in Chinese astrology, like creativity and gentleness, but it is not exactly the same as Aries.
- **Overlap and Differences**: Although Western Aries is a "fire sign" that can be quite driven, the Chinese Goat/Sheep personality is often described as kind, thoughtful, and calm. So the parallels to Aries are not exact. That said, some folks

like to combine Chinese and Western astrology to see if they notice any similarities, but this is more of a modern personal approach than a traditional practice.

## 7. Indian (Vedic) Astrology and the Aries Concept

In India, there is a long tradition of Vedic astrology, also called Jyotish. This system also divides the sky into twelve signs, similar to Western astrology, but it uses a sidereal (star-based) zodiac rather than the tropical zodiac used in the West. This means the timing of when the Sun enters Aries in Vedic astrology can differ by about 23–24 days from Western dates.

- **Name in Sanskrit**: In many Vedic astrology texts, Aries is called "Mesha," which means "ram." So there is a direct link to a ram symbol here as well.
- **Traits in Vedic Astrology**: People with Mesha as their Sun sign (or important placements) are said to be energetic, brave, and sometimes a bit impatient, much like Western Aries. Mars is also the ruler of Mesha in Vedic thought, which adds an extra layer of similarity to Western Aries.
- **Festivals and Rituals**: Since the sidereal system is used, the exact day Mesha begins can be tied to certain local events or religious observations in some parts of India. Though it may not be as widely recognized in everyday life, those who follow Vedic astrology pay attention to transitions, especially the shift from one sign to another.

## 8. Aries in Persian Traditions

In ancient Persia, astronomy and astrology were advanced fields. While modern-day Iran and nearby areas have changed over centuries, the old Persian calendars sometimes reflected aspects that lined up with the spring equinox. The start of spring was important because it signaled new life and the opening of the farming season. Although the word "Aries" might not have been used exactly, the presence of a "spring sign" associated with a horned animal or fresh starts is present in several ancient Middle Eastern traditions.

- **Nowruz (Persian New Year)**: This event marks the spring equinox. While not named for Aries, it falls around March 20 or 21, the same time the Sun often moves into Aries in Western astrology. This shows how the idea of fresh energy and rebirth at this time of year is common in many cultures, whether or not they use the specific Aries name or symbol.
- **Star-Watching Culture**: Persian astronomers also made star charts that influenced Islamic golden-age scholars. The concept of dividing the sky into sections (including the Ram) was passed through these traditions, though with different naming.

## 9. Aries in Mesoamerican and Other Indigenous Views

The Maya, Aztec, and other Mesoamerican cultures had their own calendars and star lore. They did not have "Aries" as part of their systems, but they also tracked equinoxes, eclipses, and important sky events for planting, harvest, and religious events. The group of stars we call Aries might have been seen differently, perhaps as part of another shape or pattern. In many indigenous cultures around the world, constellations do not match the Greek patterns at all.

- **Different Shapes**: One group might have seen a turtle where Greeks saw a ram. Another might have considered those stars part of a larger figure.
- **Shared Sense of Renewal**: Even if the shape is different, the time of year around late March still signals the arrival of

spring in the northern half of the Earth, which many societies mark as a time of growth and new beginnings.

While these local systems do not confirm Aries traits, they often reflect a common theme of lively energy and fresh starts, which mirrors Aries' role in Western astrology as the sign that opens the zodiac cycle.

## 10. Aries in Modern Global Context

Today, thanks to the internet, people share and learn about many kinds of astrology. Someone in East Asia might read about Western Aries, and a person in Europe might read about Vedic Mesha. This has led to a blending of ideas:

- **Hybrid Practices**: Some individuals look at both their Western Sun sign (Aries if born between late March and mid-April) and their sidereal sign in Vedic astrology. They might note differences or see how they overlap.
- **Cross-Cultural Curiosity**: People might compare Aries with the Sheep/Goat in the Chinese zodiac, or see if any local star lore in their culture matches Aries traits.
- **Online Groups**: Many websites and forums let users discuss how Aries is viewed in their country. This can be fun and educational, showing that the same star cluster can have many stories attached to it.

## 11. The Ram Image in Art and Symbolism

Across different cultures, the ram often appears in art, sculpture, and coat of arms (official symbols for families or groups). While not everyone calls it "Aries," the basic qualities people often link with rams—strength, guarding, or forceful movement—appear in these symbols. Some examples:

- **European Heraldry**: In the medieval period, knights and noble families sometimes used animals like the ram on their banners to suggest fearlessness or a will to protect.
- **African Masks**: Certain tribal art in regions of Africa includes ram horns in ceremonial masks, signifying leadership or the power of life.
- **Modern Logos**: Some sports teams or companies use a ram's head for a logo, suggesting drive and boldness, which, interestingly, matches Aries-like themes in popular culture.

## 12. Aries Festivals and Seasonal Markers

While we have to avoid a specific word for group gatherings or special events, it is worth noting that many cultures have had times of year that match or come close to the Aries date range. Around late March or early April, spring arrives in the northern half of the globe, so people in many cultures hold events welcoming warmer days. For example:

- **Northern India**: Different regions may hold spring gatherings with special foods and songs. This time can coincide with the sidereal Aries shift in Vedic astrology.
- **Middle East**: Nowruz, mentioned earlier, is observed by various groups and lines up with the spring equinox, around the start of Aries in Western terms.
- **Western Countries**: The last week of March and early April may hold local fairs or school breaks that mark the end of winter. While not always tied to Aries by name, the idea of a fresh season is in line with Aries' symbolism.

So, even though the sign "Aries" might not be named in all these events, the same time period is often recognized as a season of forward motion, warmth, and the start of planting in areas with farmland.

## 13. Spiritual or New Age Groups and Aries

In modern times, some spiritual or New Age circles have taken the concept of Aries and blended it with their own teachings. They might say that during "Aries season" (March 21–April 19 in Western astrology), the world experiences an extra dose of "fiery energy." In their view, this is a good time for new plans, for stepping out of comfort zones, or for physically re-energizing. Some might hold small group circles to focus on these Aries themes, talking about how to use the direct nature of Aries in daily life.

- **Mix of Traditions**: These groups often combine Western astrological ideas with concepts from Eastern beliefs, indigenous practices, or personal intuitions.
- **Personal Ceremonies**: A person might light a candle or write down goals during Aries season, hoping to harness the sign's spark. While this is not an ancient practice, it shows how Aries is viewed today across cultural lines, with people picking the parts that resonate.

## 14. Academic Views: Cross-Cultural Astrology Studies

Some scholars research how different cultures shaped their own star patterns and how these merged or clashed over time. Aries is a perfect example of a Greek-based figure (the Ram) that was passed down from Babylonian star lore. Researchers might compare Babylonian cuneiform tablets, Greek texts like those by Ptolemy, and Roman works to see how the Ram idea evolved. They might also look at Egyptian star maps, Islamic golden-age astronomy, and Indian Jyotish texts to understand differences and similarities.

- **Translations and Errors**: Over centuries, translations sometimes altered names or descriptions. A star called "the ram's horn" might become something else in another language.

- **Modern Astronomy vs. Astrology**: Today's astronomy sees Aries as a constellation with certain stars like Hamal, Sheratan, and Mesarthim, while astrology focuses on Aries as a zodiac sign that may not align exactly with those stars due to the precession of Earth's axis. Scholars often draw lines between practical star-watching for navigation and the more symbolic interpretation for human traits.

## 15. Aries' Reputation Around the World

Because Aries is strongly tied to Western pop culture, people in many lands have at least heard that Aries is about being direct and active. However, local beliefs differ:

- **Europe and the Americas**: Aries is often popularized in magazines and online horoscopes as the "leader" of the zodiac.
- **Asia**: Some folks might see Western Aries as interesting but still prefer local zodiac systems like the Chinese cycle or Japanese expansions of it.
- **Africa**: Although many people follow modern Western astrology, older customs might overshadow the zodiac for daily decisions. Aries might be known, but not as widely applied in some rural areas.
- **Australia and Oceania**: Since these regions have different seasonal shifts (autumn occurs during late March in the southern half of the Earth), the idea of Aries marking spring might not match local weather. Some people still enjoy the concept, but it does not line up with actual seasons.

## 16. The Ram's Horn in Ritual Objects

In some cultures, ram's horns are used in special objects. One example is the shofar, a ram's horn used in certain religious services in Judaism. While this is not tied to the zodiac sign Aries directly, the use of ram's horns for important signals or calls has a long history in parts of the Middle East. It suggests the ram's symbolic power remains strong in spiritual practices, even if it is not called "Aries."

## 17. Aries in Popular Media Worldwide

Movies, TV shows, and music from different regions sometimes reference "Aries" or use the ram symbol. Global fans might see:

- **Character Traits**: A character described as "classic Aries" might be hot-tempered, rushing into a challenge, or leading a group in a story.
- **Anime and Manga**: Japanese works sometimes assign zodiac signs to characters. Aries might be the impulsive hero or a side character with an energetic aura.
- **Comics in Europe or Latin America**: Similar patterns can appear, with Aries-themed heroes or villains showing bold behavior.

This spread of Aries imagery across pop culture can lead young fans in many countries to learn the basics of Western astrology, even if their families do not follow it.

## 18. Cross-Cultural Critiques of Aries

Not everyone sees Aries as positive. Some critics say that linking a birth time to a fixed set of traits can be limiting. Cultural critics also point out that Western astrology is just one of many systems, and treating it as universal can overshadow local star lore. Others might worry that focusing on Aries as "impulsive" or "hot-headed" can create stereotypes.

- **Balancing Act**: Many people choose to see Aries or any zodiac sign as just one lens among many. They keep their local beliefs, scientific knowledge, or personal experiences in mind rather than relying solely on star signs.

## 19. Modern Spread Through Technology

The internet has brought Aries sign memes, Instagram posts, and YouTube channels to nearly every corner of the globe. Influencers who talk about zodiac signs can have followers from countries that historically did not practice Western astrology. As a result:

- **Cultural Fusion**: A person in South Africa might read about Aries traits on a U.S.-based site, then combine it with local beliefs about rams or personal spirit animals.
- **Shared Jokes**: Aries jokes or memes poke fun at the sign's direct manner or quick anger, and fans worldwide chime in with agreement or their own stories.
- **Educational Benefit**: People are learning that there is more than one zodiac system. This helps with open-mindedness and comparison of cultural practices.

# CHAPTER 14: ARIES & LEISURE ACTIVITIES

Aries is known for its active, bold, and energetic nature. But how does that show up when Aries folks are simply enjoying themselves? Free time is not all about rest on the couch for many Aries; they often look for something stimulating or challenging to do. In this chapter, we will explore various leisure activities that might appeal to people with Aries traits. We will consider physical sports, group outings, creative hobbies, relaxation methods, and ways Aries can spend free time without feeling bored. Since Aries tends to have strong bursts of energy, we will also talk about how they might handle quieter moments when excitement dies down. This chapter aims to offer insights into how Aries might make the most of weekends, holidays, or any break from work or school.

## 1. Aries and Physical Activities

One of the most typical images of Aries is someone who loves movement. Not every Aries is a star athlete, but many do enjoy some form of exercise or competitive fun. They might get a thrill from pushing their bodies, improving their skills, and feeling the rush of adrenaline. Some popular choices include:

1. **Team Sports**: Soccer, basketball, rugby, or volleyball might all entice Aries because there is fast action, direct competition, and a chance to stand out as a leader.
2. **Racquet Sports**: Tennis, badminton, or squash can be appealing because of the quick movements and one-on-one or doubles challenge.

3. **Martial Arts**: Karate, tae kwon do, judo, or other styles might draw Aries who like discipline paired with physical effort and a test of courage.
4. **Running or Cycling**: Some Aries like the feeling of setting personal records or dashing through new trails, driven by the urge to go faster or farther.

These activities let Aries channel their fire sign energy in a healthy way, preventing restlessness from building up. They can also become social outlets, especially team sports, where Aries can show leadership and encourage others.

## 2. Enjoying Competition and Challenges

Even if Aries is not into sports, they might still crave challenges. Aries often likes the thrill of seeing who can do better—whether it is a video game contest, a puzzle race, or a friendly bet about who can finish a task first. Activities that satisfy this urge include:

- **Board Games and Strategy Games**: Aries might enjoy quick, intense games that require fast thinking. Games like chess or strategy board games can appeal if they do not drag on too long.
- **Arcade Competitions**: Old-school or modern arcades, where Aries can try to beat high scores, might give a burst of excitement.
- **Online Gaming**: Fast-paced multiplayer games, such as certain shooters or battle arenas, can keep Aries on their toes, especially if they can hop into the action without lengthy waiting.

These competitive outlets can be fun, but Aries must watch out for frustration if they lose. Keeping the mood friendly helps them enjoy the activity rather than turning it into an argument.

## 3. Outdoor Adventures and Exploration

Aries is often drawn to places or activities that bring a sense of freedom and excitement. Instead of staying home, Aries might say, "Let's go somewhere new!" Some outdoor pastimes could be:

1. **Hiking or Trekking**: Aries might enjoy a brisk walk on a scenic trail, especially if it has challenging inclines or rocky terrain. They get to test their stamina and see great views.
2. **Rock Climbing or Bouldering**: Climbing demands both physical effort and mental focus. Aries could be attracted to the challenge of scaling walls or natural cliffs.
3. **Water Sports**: Activities like kayaking, surfing, or rafting might excite Aries. The combination of physical skill and the thrill of moving water lines up well with Aries' love of action.
4. **Camping**: Setting up a tent, making a campfire, and exploring the area can engage Aries' practical side, but they might prefer short camping trips with plenty to do, rather than quiet, extended stays.

Outdoor fun provides a natural playground for Aries to burn off energy. However, they should plan sensibly, especially if the site is remote. Aries might get carried away by impulse, so double-checking safety and supplies is wise.

## 4. Aries and Group Socializing

As a fire sign, Aries can be quite social, liking the buzz of being around people. For leisure, they might propose group outings. These could be anything from visiting an amusement park to playing paintball. The key is having a chance to move and interact. Some group-based activities:

- **Theme Park Trips**: Fast rides, bright lights, and loud music can appeal to Aries' senses. They might be the first to volunteer for the most intense roller coasters.
- **Escape Rooms**: Solving puzzles under time pressure with a group can tap into Aries' competitive and team-focused side. They might take the lead, though they should remember to let others solve some clues too.
- **Dance Nights or Parties**: If Aries enjoys dancing, they might gravitate to lively music and a place where they can show off some moves.
- **Weekly Sports Leagues**: Adult leagues for soccer, basketball, or softball can blend social time with friendly competition.

Aries might find that their natural spark can get a group energized. They just need to ensure they are not dominating the plan too heavily. Sharing the spotlight with friends or family fosters a better time for everyone.

## 5. Creative Hobbies for Aries

Although physical and social activities often top Aries' list, many Aries folks also love creative outlets. They might enjoy making something new or expressing themselves in a hands-on way. Creative hobbies that can suit an Aries mindset include:

1. **Painting or Sketching**: Aries might paint bold, bright pictures or quickly capture scenes. Some Aries prefer rapid methods—like acrylics—so they can finish a piece without waiting too long for layers to dry.
2. **Pottery or Sculpting**: Working with clay or other materials can be tactile and immediate. Aries might find it satisfying to shape something right away, rather than spend hours on small details.

3. **Woodworking or DIY Projects**: Building simple furniture or doing home improvements can let Aries see quick progress. They might relish using tools, as it aligns with the direct approach of "doing" instead of just thinking.
4. **Writing and Storytelling**: Some Aries are drawn to writing short, impactful pieces—blog posts, poems, or short stories. They might not want to settle into a long novel, but they can pour out strong ideas quickly.

For Aries, the key is often immediacy: something that shows results soon. Long, slow projects that drag out for months might make them impatient. Breaking large tasks into smaller chunks could keep Aries engaged.

## 6. Traveling for Fun

Seeing new places can feed Aries' desire for fresh experiences. They might not always plan trips in detail, preferring to go with the flow once they arrive. Some Aries might love:

- **Short Weekend Getaways**: Aries does not need a huge, drawn-out trip. A quick run to a nearby city, beach, or mountainside might be enough to recharge their sense of adventure.
- **Active Vacations**: Instead of lying around a pool all day, Aries might sign up for zip-lining, mountain biking, or city tours that involve a lot of walking.
- **Road Trips**: Aries can enjoy the thrill of driving on open roads, stopping whenever they spot something interesting. They might not schedule every stop, leaving room for discovery.

Being mindful of finances and safety is important. Aries might get carried away with the excitement of going places, so setting a basic budget and route is wise.

## 7. Quick-Fix Pastimes for Aries

Sometimes, Aries only has a little bit of free time—maybe an hour after work or a free afternoon on the weekend. Because they often do not like to sit idle, they might look for short, intense activities such as:

- **Mobile Gaming**: Fast, competitive games on a phone can fill a short break. Aries might choose puzzle games with timers or quick platformers that get the heart racing.
- **Fitness Challenges**: A 30-minute high-intensity workout or a local 5K fun run can give them an adrenaline boost.
- **Cooking Sprints**: Aries may try cooking something bold but quick. They might enjoy throwing together spicy recipes or experimenting with flavors on the fly.

These bite-sized pastimes allow Aries to stay busy and keep boredom away, even if time is tight.

## 8. Aries and Relaxation Methods

Though Aries is full of energy, they still need rest to prevent burnout. Some Aries folks find typical relaxation—like sitting quietly—tough. However, there are ways for Aries to rest without feeling restless:

1. **Active Relaxation**: Light yoga, stretching routines, or gentle walks in nature can calm an Aries mind while letting them move a bit.
2. **Listening to Music**: Some Aries feel recharged by lively, upbeat tunes. Others might need calmer music if their day was hectic.
3. **Short Mindful Breathing**: Taking even two or three minutes to breathe slowly can lower stress. Aries does not have to spend an hour meditating; a short session might be enough.

4. **Creative Daydreaming**: Sometimes, Aries can rest their body while letting their mind wander about new ideas or future plans, turning it into a gentle form of relaxation.

Finding the right balance between activity and calm is key. Aries who never slow down can burn out. A small daily rest session can keep that from happening.

## 9. Social Media and Online Activities

Aries might also use free time on social platforms, whether posting pictures, chatting with friends, or following trending topics. Their straightforward style can show up in how they comment or share. They might also enjoy:

- **Short Video Platforms**: Quick bursts of funny or exciting content can match Aries' short attention span.
- **Online Challenges**: Aries might join in viral challenges, trying to beat or top others' attempts.
- **Digital Creation**: Some Aries run their own channels or blogs, posting fast takes on events, games, or personal opinions. They like immediate reactions, such as likes or comments.

However, Aries might need to watch for online arguments. Their direct approach can spark heated debates, so stepping away before things get too intense is wise.

## 10. Aries with Family Leisure

When spending free time with family members—especially if there are kids or older relatives—Aries might need to adapt. Some family-friendly ideas:

- **Garden Projects**: Aries can help kids dig small garden plots or plant flowers. It is a chance to move around and see quick results if it is a fast-growing plant.
- **Simple Crafts**: If the family includes younger children, Aries can guide them in easy crafts or painting.
- **Outdoor Picnics**: Aries might enjoy organizing an outdoor meal with simple games like frisbee or small ball toss for everyone.
- **Storytelling Nights**: Aries who like drama can gather the family to tell short, exciting stories or read a lively book aloud. They can act out characters, which can be fun for kids.

Balancing the different energy levels in a family may require patience. Aries might want to do something very active, but a grandparent or toddler might not keep up. Mixing calmer activities with short bursts of movement can work well.

## 11. Aries and Solo Time

Although Aries is often social, they might still value moments alone, especially to think up new ideas. What might Aries do alone?

- **Journaling**: Aries can jot down quick thoughts about the day or any upcoming plans. It allows them to clarify what they want to do next.
- **Learning New Skills**: Aries might watch tutorial videos on a new hobby, like playing guitar or doing a basic magic trick. They may enjoy the challenge of mastering something fresh.
- **Late-Night Walks**: Some Aries find a short nighttime stroll helps them settle their mind before sleep.

Being alone can help Aries listen to their inner voice without outside noise. Even short solo breaks can recharge them, preventing them from feeling overwhelmed by constant group activities.

## 12. Aries and Performance Arts

Some Aries flourish when they can perform for an audience—whether that means acting, singing, or playing an instrument. Performance hobbies that Aries might take on:

- **Theater Groups**: Local theater allows Aries to express strong emotions on stage. They might play roles that show confidence or dramatic flair.
- **Improv Comedy**: Quick thinking, audience interaction, and the adrenaline of being on the spot can fit well with Aries' boldness.
- **Music Bands**: Aries might pick up a rock instrument like guitar or drums, or they might enjoy singing lead vocals if they have the voice for it. They get to show energy and connect with fans.

Performing can be thrilling but also requires practice. Aries might need to work on staying committed, not jumping to a new interest too soon.

## 13. Building Close Friendships Through Shared Leisure

Aries can deepen friendships by sharing activities. Doing something exciting together can create strong bonds. Examples:

- **Challenge Buddies**: Aries might form a pact with a friend to tackle new tasks regularly, like weekly rock-climbing sessions or puzzle challenges.
- **Volunteer Projects**: Aries who want to give back might do local volunteer work. Building a community garden or painting a community center can be both active and meaningful.

- **Travel Partners**: If Aries finds a friend with a similar style, they can take short road trips or sign up for adventurous tours.

Shared leisure not only keeps Aries busy but also helps them develop trust and teamwork with friends, adding a social dimension to their free time.

## 14. Easing Restlessness After the Thrill

Aries often feels a "crash" after excitement. Suppose they have spent the day on a thrilling outing or a competitive event. That night or the next day, they might feel restless if nothing new is happening. Strategies to cope:

- **Mini-Recharge**: Plan a small follow-up treat, like a favorite snack or a short online chat with friends, to keep spirits up.
- **Switch Focus**: If the big event is done, focus on a smaller project or a chore that needs doing, to avoid feeling empty. Aries can still keep moving, just at a gentler pace.
- **Plan the Next Activity**: Aries can set up the next adventure on the calendar, so they have something to look forward to, even if it is a few weeks away.

This can help Aries avoid a slump and maintain steady emotional health between bursts of intense fun.

## 15. Aries and Reading or Learning for Fun

Not all Aries prefer reading, but those who do might lean toward certain types of books or courses:

- **Action-Packed Fiction**: Stories that move quickly, with heroes facing big challenges, can keep Aries turning pages.

- **Biographies of Bold Figures**: Aries might be inspired by true stories of explorers, adventurers, or inventors who took risks.
- **Skill-Based Books**: Manuals on photography, coding, or a new sport might spark Aries' desire to learn and apply.
- **Short Online Courses**: Aries could sign up for a short digital class if it promises tangible results—like learning a new design tool—in a brief time.

Reading for Aries might be an active pursuit: they often want to do something with the knowledge right away.

## 16. Aries and Gatherings

If Aries organizes a home gathering for friends or family, they might plan something lively and interactive:

- **Game Night**: Aries might choose high-energy games or quick rounds of trivia so no one gets bored.
- **Cooking Together**: Aries could set up a "cook-off" or a pizza-making station. They enjoy activities where everyone is doing something.
- **Backyard Sports**: If there is enough space, Aries might host a mini-tournament of badminton, table tennis, or a basketball shootout.
- **Music and Dancing**: Aries might put together a fun playlist and encourage guests to dance or sing karaoke.

Their direct style can help them coordinate tasks, though they should be careful not to boss others around. Letting everyone have a say can ensure a smooth, enjoyable time.

## 17. Managing Downtime When Friends Are Busy

There may be times when Aries wants to do something active, but friends or family are tied up. What can Aries do alone to not feel bored?

- **Self-Challenges**: They can set a personal challenge, like learning five new dance moves from online tutorials in an afternoon.
- **Home Projects**: Aries might paint a room in the house, build a shelf, or rearrange furniture for a fresh look. This physical effort keeps them busy and yields visible results.
- **Online Communities**: Aries can join communities or forums about hobbies they like. They might swap tips or compete virtually, keeping that sense of connection going.

By finding ways to self-motivate, Aries does not have to rely on others to have a good time.

## 18. Aries and Nature Exploration

While we touched on outdoorsy fun, some Aries also enjoy simple nature visits:

- **Nature Photography**: Aries with a camera might snap quick shots of interesting spots, insects, or birds. Trying to capture the perfect image can feel like a mission.
- **Picnics with Action**: Instead of a calm picnic, Aries might pick a spot by a lake or near hiking trails, so there is something to do after eating.
- **Guided Wildlife Tours**: If Aries is curious about animals, they might join a safari-style tour (if possible) or a local nature reserve walk.

These activities feed Aries' active mind while letting them enjoy fresh air and scenic views.

## 19. Budget-Friendly Leisure for Aries

Excitement does not have to be expensive. Aries can have fun without draining their wallet:

- **Local Sports Courts**: Many neighborhoods have free public courts for basketball, tennis, or even skate parks. Aries can head there with a friend.
- **Free Workshops or Classes**: Community centers sometimes offer short lessons in dance, art, or other skills. Aries can jump in if it sounds interesting.
- **Household Tournaments**: Aries can set up a mini-competition at home with simple tasks (like who can fold laundry faster, or who can do more push-ups). This might sound silly, but it can bring laughter and friendly rivalry.
- **Online Tutorials**: Many how-to videos are free, so Aries can learn a new craft or cooking recipe at zero cost.

By using creativity, Aries can keep their leisure exciting without worrying about large bills or fancy gear.

# CHAPTER 15: ARIES & PERSONAL GOALS

Aries is often linked to boldness, directness, and eagerness to start new projects. One key aspect of this sign is how strongly it pursues goals. Aries tends to be action-based and likes to see results quickly, which can help them reach successes in many areas—school, work, fitness, creative tasks, or personal projects. Yet, the same Aries traits can also cause hurdles, such as impatience or a lack of follow-through. In this chapter, we will explore how Aries may set, track, and achieve personal goals in different parts of life. We will talk about helpful strategies to stay motivated, avoid burnout, and build steady progress. By learning to harness Aries' natural fire in a balanced way, people of this sign can gain a sense of satisfaction and direction that aligns with their high energy.

## 1. Why Aries Thrives on Goals

Aries, being a fire sign, loves to feel that spark of excitement when starting something new. When Aries has a clear purpose, it can charge forward with plenty of drive. Goals give Aries a direction to channel that energy. Without a sense of aim, Aries may feel restless or bored, leading to frustration or jumping between random tasks. Having a target—big or small—allows Aries to wake up thinking, "Let's do this!" and to maintain the unstoppable vibe that often defines this sign.

In addition, Aries folks tend to enjoy competition, even if it is just competing with themselves. Setting a goal can create a personal challenge: "I want to improve my math grade," "I want to run faster," or "I want to launch a small business idea." Achieving milestones feels satisfying, like winning a mini-contest or finishing a race. This sense of ongoing challenge can keep Aries' spirit alive.

## 2. Types of Goals Aries Might Set

Everyone has unique aims, but Aries usually seeks goals that involve direct action, visible progress, or some measure of risk or daring. Some examples:

- **Physical and Fitness Goals**: Aries might aim to run a certain distance, lift heavier weights, improve in a sport, or learn a new exercise routine. Physical aims fit Aries' love for movement and quick results.
- **Career and School Goals**: Aries might plan to finish assignments faster, reach a certain grade, or land a leadership role at work. They thrive on tasks that allow them to see progress soon, so short-term achievements can be especially motivating.
- **Creative Goals**: Painting a series of pictures, writing a short story, crafting a set of handmade items, or starting a YouTube channel. Aries may enjoy the challenge of producing something original and sharing it.
- **Personal Life Goals**: Aries might want to become more confident in social settings, learn to handle anger calmly, or build better daily habits. These personal development goals allow Aries to refine its fiery traits into something more polished.

In each case, Aries typically wants at least a portion of the goal to be measurable or immediate, so they can see that the effort is paying off.

## 3. Short-Term vs. Long-Term Goals

Aries naturally leans toward short-term goals because these match the sign's desire for quick outcomes. Whether it is deciding to improve the time in a 5K run or finishing an upcoming project by the end of the week, shorter aims feed Aries' excitement. Long-term plans, such as saving money for a big purchase or training for a year-long certification, can be more challenging. Aries might lose interest if there are no visible results along the way.

- **Short-Term Goals**:
    - Easy to keep the spark alive.
    - Provide quick wins that boost motivation.
    - Fit Aries' "go now" style.
- **Long-Term Goals**:
    - Require ongoing patience.
    - Might lead to boredom if Aries cannot see steady progress.
    - Demand breaking down into small parts to remain interesting.

A good approach for Aries is to combine both. For instance, if Aries has a one-year goal of completing an advanced skill course, they can divide it into monthly targets or short projects that each offer a sense of success. This way, Aries gets the thrill of achieving something regularly while still moving toward the bigger picture.

## 4. Setting Effective Goals: Aries-Friendly Tips

1. **Be Specific and Bold**: Aries tends to respond to clear, challenging aims. "I want to get better grades" is less powerful than "I want to raise my math grade from a C to a B by the next report." Aries will enjoy the directness and the sense of pushing boundaries.

2. **Add a Time Frame**: "I will finish writing three short stories by the end of the month" triggers Aries' urgency. The sign thrives when there is a ticking clock that calls for quick action.
3. **Allow Room for Flexibility**: Aries is impulsive and might discover new interests mid-way. Goals should be focused but not overly rigid. If a new, beneficial opportunity arises, Aries can adjust rather than feeling trapped.
4. **Choose Something That Sparks Excitement**: If a goal feels dull, Aries may abandon it. Aries does best when the aim lights a fire inside, whether it is an intense challenge, a chance to learn, or a unique way to stand out.

## 5. Maintaining Momentum

Aries often starts strong but may fade if the path gets repetitive. This can lead to half-done projects. To keep momentum, Aries can:

- *Celebrate Small Wins*: Mark each mini-success—like finishing a chapter of a personal project or running a faster mile time. Aries loves recognition, even self-recognition, though we will avoid a certain term.
- **Switch It Up**: If Aries is bored with the same routine, try a fresh angle. For a fitness goal, vary the workouts. For a creative goal, change tools or mediums. This keeps the mind engaged.
- **Check Progress Often**: Aries can benefit from short weekly reviews. How much closer are they to the goal? What got done this week? This can refuel the desire to keep going.

A steady trickle of interesting tasks, mini-accomplishments, and variety helps Aries remain committed beyond that initial burst of enthusiasm.

# 6. Handling Obstacles and Setbacks

No matter how strong the initial drive is, every Aries might face obstacles—unexpected events, limited time, or simply feeling tired. Because Aries can have a quick temper or feel impatient, these setbacks might be met with anger or frustration. Strategies to handle this:

1. **Pause Before Reacting**: Aries can learn to take a brief break when hitting a roadblock. This might be a short walk, a few deep breaths, or talking it out with a friend. Cooling down can prevent rash decisions.
2. **Review the Original Plan**: Maybe the plan was too tight or lacked a backup. Aries can fine-tune the goal or the approach instead of quitting altogether.
3. **Stay Solution-Focused**: Instead of dwelling on the problem, Aries can ask, "What's the next best step?" This aligns with Aries' action-oriented nature, turning frustration into forward movement.
4. **Use Support**: Friends, mentors, or loved ones can help Aries keep perspective. Sharing the setback might reveal new ideas. Because Aries likes independence, it can be hard to ask for help, but outside viewpoints can be invaluable.

Setbacks do not have to end the plan. Aries can use each challenge as fuel to keep going with fresh tactics.

# 7. Balancing Competitive Drive

Aries often thrives on healthy competition—sometimes with others, sometimes with themselves. However, too much competition can turn a goal into an unhealthy rivalry, straining relationships and causing stress. Aries can watch out for signs that competition is becoming negative, such as:

- Always comparing outcomes to others in a bitter way.
- Feeling upset if a friend or coworker does better.
- Focusing on beating someone rather than reaching personal growth.

To keep competition helpful, Aries might set personal standards. It is fine to be inspired by someone else's success, but the real measure of growth should be personal improvement. This mindset fosters positive energy while still satisfying Aries' urge to push forward.

## 8. Reward Systems That Fit Aries

Because Aries likes immediate excitement, setting up small rewards can boost morale. These rewards can be simple or creative:

- **Fun Activities**: After reaching a certain milestone, Aries can treat themselves to a short outing, like playing a favorite sport or watching a new movie at home.
- **Upgrade Gear**: If working on a creative or fitness goal, a small gear upgrade (like new art supplies or better running shoes) can feel like progress.
- **Social Sharing**: Aries can share a milestone on social media or with close friends. Hearing "Well done!" from others can motivate Aries to keep going.
- **Relaxation**: Sometimes, the best reward is a bit of rest—like a calming bath or a lazy evening reading a book.

The key is to keep these rewards balanced, so Aries does not rely entirely on external treats, but they still get a motivational push to stay on track.

## 9. Time Management for Aries

Time management can be tricky for Aries because the sign may jump at new tasks and shift focus quickly. Yet, to meet goals, Aries needs some level of structure.

- **Create Short Work Sessions**: Aries might do best in focused bursts—30 minutes or an hour of intense effort, followed by a short break. This approach harnesses Aries' energy without draining it.
- **Use Visual Tools**: Aries can keep a calendar or a colorful chart to see deadlines. If it is fun or visually striking, Aries is more likely to check it often.
- **Prioritize**: Aries might want to do many things at once. Listing tasks by importance ensures the most critical parts are done first, avoiding a panic rush later.
- **Set Clear Start Times**: Because Aries is impulsive, they may begin tasks at random. Having a set time to start each day's major goal can form a habit, making it easier to stick with the plan.

Consistent use of time helps Aries make real progress instead of scattering energy across too many interests.

## 10. Dealing with the "Middle Slump"

It is common for Aries to feel a "slump" in the middle of a project or goal. The first rush fades, and the final outcome feels far away. Aries might think, "This is boring now," or "I want something new." To push through:

1. **Refresh the Vision**: Aries can visualize how good it will feel to reach the final target. Reminding themselves why they started can reignite the flame.

2. **Add a Twist**: If the routine is dull, changing a step can spice things up. For instance, if Aries is studying for an exam, they could try a new study partner or a different location.
3. **Break It Down**: Setting smaller goals within the bigger goal can show progress. For a big writing project, Aries might aim for a certain number of pages or sections each week.
4. **Seek Encouragement**: Talking to someone who believes in the Aries dream can spark fresh motivation. Aries might also look at past successes to recall how they overcame slumps before.

The middle slump is normal; with a bit of creativity, Aries can push past it and rediscover their drive.

## 11. Staying Organized Without Losing Spontaneity

Aries often resists rigid routines, fearing they will lose the freedom to act on impulse. However, some organization is crucial for serious goals. The trick is to balance structure with flexibility:

- **Loose Schedules**: Aries can plan broad time blocks instead of every minute. For example, "Morning for writing, afternoon for errands, evening for fitness." This leaves some wiggle room.
- **Focus on Outcomes**: Aries might track results instead of strictly scheduling how to get them. For instance, "By Wednesday, I want 10 pages drafted," and how they do that is flexible.
- **Keep Some Free Slots**: Having open segments in the week to handle sudden interests or tasks can let Aries explore spontaneous ideas without derailing the main plan.

By thinking of schedules as helpful guidelines instead of prison walls, Aries can get the best of both worlds.

## 12. Personal Growth Goals for Aries Traits

Not all goals are about sports, school, or career. Aries might also want to shape personal habits or emotional patterns. For instance:

1. **Patience Goals**: Aries can aim to pause before reacting in tense moments. They might track how often they manage to stay calm in a week.
2. **Listening Skills**: An Aries who wants better relationships might practice letting others speak first in a conversation. They can measure success by how the talk flows.
3. **Thoughtful Spending**: Aries can learn to pause before making impulsive buys, giving themselves a day to think.
4. **Time With Loved Ones**: If Aries tends to be busy, they can set a goal for weekly quality moments with friends or family.

These personal growth targets might be less tangible but can deeply enhance Aries' life by balancing out the sign's intense side.

## 13. Group Goals and Aries Leadership

Sometimes, Aries works toward a shared aim with family, friends, or coworkers—like a group project, a fundraiser, or a volunteer event. Aries might step into a leadership role naturally. Strategies to succeed:

- **Use Aries Energy Wisely**: Aries can ignite the group by showing confidence and a fast start. That can pull hesitant members along.
- **Listen to Feedback**: Aries must remember that not everyone moves at the same speed. Let others voice ideas to avoid friction.
- **Set Clear Milestones**: Break the shared goal into small tasks. Aries can keep the team on track by celebrating each success (in a modest way) and pushing for the next.

- **Prevent Burnout**: Aries may try to do everything alone. Instead, delegate tasks, trusting that the group can help. This fosters teamwork and keeps Aries from feeling overloaded.

Leading group goals can be rewarding for Aries, as they can channel their natural boldness while learning vital cooperation skills.

## 14. Technology Tools to Help Aries

In modern times, many apps and platforms can boost goal-setting:

- **Task Apps**: Aries can use simple to-do apps that let them check off finished items quickly, appealing to the sign's love of instant feedback.
- **Timer Apps**: The Pomodoro Technique or other timed-focus methods can help Aries stay engaged.
- **Habit Trackers**: A daily streak of small actions—like reading or doing push-ups—can keep Aries motivated, as they see the streak build.
- **Online Groups**: Aries might join online challenge groups to share progress with people who have similar aims. The sense of competition or camaraderie can keep that spark going.

Aries should choose tools that feel active and straightforward. Overly complicated systems might lead to frustration or neglect.

## 15. Celebrating the Finish Line and Next Steps

When Aries does reach the end of a goal—whether it is finishing a big art piece or hitting a new personal record at the gym—there is a great sense of triumph. It is important for Aries to take a moment to mark the achievement, even if the sign usually rushes to the next project. That might look like:

- **Sharing the Success Story**: Telling close friends, posting a photo, or writing a short reflection helps Aries recognize the work they put in.
- **Reflecting on Lessons Learned**: Aries might do a quick review: What worked best? What will they try next time? This forms a base for bigger achievements.
- **Brief Rest**: Aries could schedule a day off from that activity to let the mind and body recharge. This prevents immediate burnout before jumping into the next big thing.

Shortly after finishing, Aries might already feel eager for a new challenge. That is a natural part of the Aries spirit—always wanting the next mountain to climb. However, balancing excitement with a brief pause can ensure sustained health and happiness.

## 16. Facing Fear of Failure or Success

Aries can appear confident, but deep inside, some Aries folks might fear that they will not meet their own high standards or might worry about what happens if they do too well and face even bigger expectations. Both fears can block progress. Approaches to handle these worries:

- **Step-by-Step Mindset**: Instead of thinking about the entire outcome, Aries can focus on the next small goal. This shrinks fear because each step feels manageable.
- **Normalize Mistakes**: Remind Aries that errors are part of growth. A mistake is not the end, but a clue on how to improve.
- **Embrace Success Gradually**: If Aries achieves a big win, they can celebrate quietly, reflect on how to keep going, and remember they do not have to do everything alone.

- **Talk to Mentors**: Trusted mentors or friends can share stories of their own setbacks and successes. Aries might realize these are normal patterns.

By seeing both failure and success as natural stops on the path, Aries can approach goals with more freedom and less stress.

## 17. Teaching Young Aries About Goals

If a parent or teacher works with an Aries child or teen on goal-setting:

1. **Keep It Fun**: Tie the goal to something the child already enjoys. If they like soccer, set a target for scoring a certain number of goals in practice or improving dribbling skills.
2. **Use Visual Tools**: A chart or star system might help younger Aries see progress.
3. **Short and Direct**: Kids often have limited attention. Simple tasks like "Read for 15 minutes" or "Finish three math problems" fit well.
4. **Praise Effort**: Aries kids love to hear positive feedback about their action. Even if the result is not perfect, praising the attempt can fuel them to keep trying.

Teaching Aries youngsters how to manage goals early sets them up for future success in more complex tasks.

## 18. Pairing Goals with Personal Values

Aries is not just about action—it also has a warm side that cares about fairness or helping others. Linking personal goals to deeper values can give them extra meaning. For instance:

- **Social Impact**: Aries who care about a cause might aim to raise funds, lead a community clean-up, or start a campaign.

The result is not only personal satisfaction but also helping others.

- **Family and Friends**: Maybe Aries wants to plan a small gathering or do something to support a friend's needs. That sense of caring can fuel the Aries drive.
- **Health and Well-Being**: An Aries might make a goal to live more healthily (like balanced eating or mindful breaks) because they value feeling strong and energetic.

When Aries aligns goals with what truly matters to them, the likelihood of follow-through increases. The heart and the fire sign's spark work together.

## 19. What Happens After One Goal Ends?

After Aries finishes a goal, there can be a short "let-down" period—sometimes Aries might feel bored because the big push is over. Aries can handle this by:

- **Resting and Reflecting**: Give time to appreciate the effort and what was learned. Then, see if any next-step goals form naturally.
- **Scaling Up**: If the project can go further, Aries might choose a bigger version. For example, if they ran a 5K, they might try to train for a 10K next.
- **Shifting Focus**: Aries might pick a fresh area altogether, like learning a new skill, if the old aim feels fully complete.
- **Helping Others**: Sometimes, Aries can guide a friend with a similar goal. Teaching or mentoring can keep Aries' spark alive while also giving them a break from personal striving.

This approach helps Aries avoid drifting and ensures that they keep feeling purposeful after hitting a milestone.

# CHAPTER 16: OVERCOMING ARIES CHALLENGES

Aries is known for fiery energy, direct speech, and a strong will. These traits can lead to incredible accomplishments and exciting relationships. However, like any sign, Aries also faces challenges—some that come from within (such as impatience or temper) and some that arise from how others react to Aries' style. In this chapter, we will look at the common hurdles Aries might encounter in day-to-day life, personal growth, and interactions with others. We will discuss practical ways to handle these difficulties so that Aries' natural spark can shine in a positive, constructive manner. By acknowledging where potential problems lie and adopting methods to address them, Aries can turn tough spots into learning points, becoming even more effective and fulfilled.

## 1. Recognizing Aries Challenges

Before we explore solutions, it is good to identify the main issues Aries can face:

1. **Quick Temper**: Aries can become annoyed or angry faster than some other signs, especially when faced with delays or unfairness.
2. **Impatience**: This sign prefers immediate action and might get restless if things move slowly.
3. **Short Attention Span**: Aries may lose interest after the initial excitement wanes, causing unfinished tasks.
4. **Overconfidence**: Believing they can handle everything alone can lead to missed warnings or burnout.

5. **Difficulty Listening**: Aries might focus on pushing forward their own ideas, sometimes overlooking input from others.

Each challenge has both a bright side and a dark side. For instance, a quick temper is tied to Aries' protective nature, and impatience stems from a desire to see results. Handling these traits carefully can keep them from causing bigger problems.

## 2. Managing the Quick Temper

Aries is passionate, which can be wonderful in many cases but can also ignite anger in an instant. Whether it is a traffic jam, a slow coworker, or a sudden disagreement, Aries might blow up quickly. Some ways to control that temper:

1. **Pause for a Breather**: Even 10 seconds of slow breathing can dampen the urge to lash out. Aries can think, "Inhale deeply, count to five, exhale, count to five." This simple act can make a big difference.
2. **Use "I" Language**: Instead of shouting, "You never listen!" Aries can say, "I feel ignored when I'm not heard." This approach lowers aggression and focuses on feelings, not blame.
3. **Step Away**: If the situation is heated, Aries can leave the room or area for a short moment. A quick walk or even a run can release that boiling energy safely.
4. **Identify the Trigger**: Over time, Aries can track what triggers anger most often (lack of control, waiting, feeling unfairly treated). Being aware lets them prepare mentally, maybe by planning to respond calmly in known hot spots.

Learning to spot anger early and defusing it is a key step. It does not remove the Aries passion but channels it more gently, preserving relationships and personal calm.

## 3. Battling Impatience

Aries thrives on swift progress and can grow upset if forced to wait. Long lines, slow decision-makers, or detailed tasks may cause Aries to fidget or speak harshly. To cope with impatience:

- **Distraction Technique**: When stuck waiting, Aries might do a quick mental game, plan the next day, or read a short article on the phone. Keeping the mind occupied prevents the rise of annoyance.
- **Plan A, Plan B**: If Aries knows a process will be slow (like waiting for official paperwork), they can bring a secondary task or an interesting book. This sense of being productive helps them feel less stuck.
- **Practice Realistic Timelines**: If Aries sets unrealistic deadlines, they will always feel behind. Learning to pad the schedule for potential delays can reduce stress.
- **Celebrate Small Steps**: When a project is lengthy, Aries can break it down into multiple stages. Each stage's finish can bring a sense of progress, easing the impatience.

By recognizing that not everything can happen at top speed, Aries might find it easier to handle the natural pace of life without constant irritation.

## 4. Finishing What Is Started

Aries loves new beginnings but can abandon projects midway if the thrill is gone. This can leave many incomplete tasks and a sense of guilt. Strategies to ensure follow-through:

1. **Public Commitment**: Telling friends or posting updates can push Aries to keep going because they do not want to appear as if they gave up.

2. **Short Sprints**: For big endeavors, work in small bursts. Each burst provides a mini-completion, which Aries can find motivating.
3. **Keep It Fresh**: Change the method or environment if boredom seeps in. If Aries is writing a report, they might move to a café or switch to a voice recording once in a while.
4. **Remember the Why**: Aries can remind themselves of the original excitement or the purpose behind the project, which can relight that initial spark.

Finishing tasks can be as thrilling as starting them, especially once Aries develops the habit of seeing the end product. The sense of pride from a completed goal can become a new fuel source.

## 5. Avoiding Overconfidence and Burnout

Aries might think: "I can handle it, no problem," then pile on more tasks than they can manage. This can lead to mistakes, stress, or even health problems. Ways to stay balanced:

- **Limit the Task Load**: Aries can pick the most important priorities rather than saying "yes" to everything. Quality often outshines quantity.
- **Check-In With the Body**: Signs of burnout might be trouble sleeping, constant tiredness, or feeling overly cranky. Aries should not ignore these.
- **Ask for Help**: Delegation or seeking advice is not weakness. Colleagues, friends, or family can share the load, allowing Aries to maintain momentum without crashing.
- **Plan Recovery Time**: After a big push, schedule rest days or calmer periods. Aries may resist resting, but it is vital for long-term energy.

Overconfidence can power Aries at first, but humility and wise planning keep them from hitting walls. Accepting that all humans have limits can help Aries maintain their spark in a healthier way.

## 6. Listening and Teamwork

Aries can be so focused on pushing a plan that they forget to check if others have ideas or concerns. This might create tension if people feel ignored. Strategies to be a better listener:

1. **Active Listening**: Look at the speaker, nod occasionally, and ask clarifying questions. Aries can confirm they heard the person: "So you're saying we should adjust the timeline?"
2. **Count to Three**: Before jumping in with a counter-idea, Aries can let the other person speak three sentences or complete their main thought. This short pause ensures they are truly heard.
3. **Value Differences**: Recognize that others bring unique insights. Another approach might solve a problem Aries never considered.
4. **Ask for Feedback**: Aries can directly request others' opinions: "What do you think about this approach?" People are more likely to share if they feel Aries is genuinely interested.

Good teamwork can multiply Aries' effectiveness. By blending Aries' boldness with other viewpoints, the result can be stronger and more harmonious.

## 7. Handling Criticism

Aries might react sharply to critiques. Because Aries invests passion into projects or decisions, a negative comment can sting. However, handling feedback gracefully is crucial:

- **Pause the Reaction**: Instead of snapping, Aries can try to understand the critique. Is it valid? Is it given in a helpful tone?
- **Separate Personal from Project**: A critique of a job or idea is not always a personal attack. Aries can step back and see if the feedback could improve the outcome.
- **Ask Questions**: Aries might say, "Can you show me what part you would change?" This moves the focus to fixing the issue.
- **Thank the Person**: Even if Aries does not agree fully, saying, "Thanks for sharing your thoughts," can keep the conversation calm and show maturity.

Taking criticism in stride makes Aries more open to growth, earning respect from those around them.

---

## 8. Calming the Aries Mind

Aries is known for a busy mind that constantly looks for the next challenge. This can hamper focus or lead to anxiety. Some calming methods:

1. **Short Relaxation Techniques**: Simple breathing exercises, quiet stretches, or guided audio for a few minutes can slow the mind without feeling like a chore.
2. **Creative Outlets**: Painting, journaling, or playing a musical instrument can provide a space to channel restless thoughts.
3. **Physical Release**: Since Aries is active, a quick jog or a set of push-ups can settle the nerves, allowing clearer thinking afterward.
4. **Steady Routines**: A short morning or bedtime routine can anchor Aries in calm habits, reducing mental chaos.

A calmer mind does not weaken Aries' spark. Instead, it provides a stable base from which that fire can burn brighter and more purposefully.

## 9. Overcoming Emotional Ups and Downs

Aries emotions can be intense, swinging between excitement and frustration. We covered anger in detail earlier, but Aries may also face sadness or disappointment strongly, sometimes masking it with outward bravado. To handle emotional swings:

- **Name the Feeling**: When Aries feels uneasy, they can ask themselves, "Am I sad, anxious, or just restless?" Naming it helps find the right fix.
- **Talk Openly**: Sharing deeper feelings with a close friend, family member, or therapist can stop Aries from bottling it all up.
- **Try Small Mood Lifters**: Music, a favorite snack, or a funny video might lighten the mood. Aries should have a few quick mood boosters ready.
- **Set Boundaries**: If certain situations or people trigger negative emotions too often, Aries can set limits or address the problem more directly.

Emotional health is about noticing feelings early and acting gently, rather than letting them explode or remain hidden.

## 10. Dealing with Delays and Bureaucracy

From time to time, everyone faces official paperwork, waiting for approvals, or dealing with slow systems that Aries cannot speed up by force of will. Tips to cope:

1. **Plan Ahead**: If Aries knows it takes weeks to get a permit or certain document, they can start the process early instead of last minute.
2. **Divide the Task**: If there are forms to fill or steps to complete, break them into small steps and tackle one at a time.
3. **Expect the Delay**: Mentally preparing for a longer wait can reduce frustration when it happens. Aries can use the downtime for other tasks.
4. **Channel Energy Elsewhere**: If Aries is forced to wait, they might use that period to brainstorm new ideas or polish existing work, maintaining a sense of progress.

Accepting that not everything moves at Aries speed can help avoid constant annoyance with red tape or official protocols.

---

## 11. Navigating Relationships with Slower-Paced Individuals

Aries might have friends, family, or partners who think and act at a gentler pace. This can lead to misunderstandings if Aries pushes too fast. Communication tips:

- **Allow More Time for Decisions**: If Aries is planning with someone who needs reflection, set a date to decide, rather than demanding an instant answer.

- **Show Patience**: Slower folks might feel rushed or disrespected if Aries is constantly hurrying them. Aries can reassure them that their comfort is also important.
- **Meet in the Middle**: For outings or tasks, Aries could propose options that have both active elements (to satisfy Aries) and calmer parts (for the other person).
- **Avoid Unnecessary Pressure**: Not all tasks require immediate action. Aries can learn to let small things be slow if it does not cause big harm.

Through understanding, Aries can build stronger bonds with different personality types and enjoy a variety of experiences.

---

## 12. Setting Realistic Expectations

Aries often imagines grand successes quickly. While this can fuel ambition, it might also create disappointment if real life does not catch up right away. Steps to set achievable goals:

- **Check Resources**: Aries might want to confirm they have the needed time, money, or knowledge before jumping in.
- **Start with a Pilot**: Test an idea on a small scale. If it goes well, scale up. If not, adjust. This approach prevents big letdowns.
- **Consider Other People's Limits**: If a project needs teamwork, Aries should ask if everyone can handle the proposed pace.
- **Celebrate Each Stage**: Mark smaller achievements along the path to a big dream, so Aries feels satisfied rather than waiting for one huge outcome.

Realistic expectations do not mean aiming low; they simply keep Aries from overextending and then feeling frustrated.

## 13. Easing Conflict in Groups

When working in teams, Aries' direct nature might spark clashes. How to reduce friction:

- **Read the Room**: Notice if people look uncomfortable or quiet. Aries might need to slow down or invite them to speak.
- **Compromise**: Aries can pick a few "must-have" points and be flexible on others, showing they value everyone's input.
- **Use Calm Tone**: Even if Aries feels strongly, a measured voice can help the group stay on track rather than escalate.
- **Assign Clear Roles**: If Aries leads, define each person's job so no one feels trampled or left out.

A bit of diplomacy can channel Aries' leadership into successful collaborations instead of power struggles.

## 14. Growing Through Mistakes

Aries moves quickly, so mistakes can happen along the way—maybe an overlooked detail or a hasty agreement. Learning from errors is crucial:

1. **Own It**: Instead of blaming others, Aries can say, "I messed up. Let's fix it." This direct admission can build trust.
2. **Search for Causes**: Was the mistake due to rushing, not checking facts, or ignoring advice? Identifying the root helps prevent repeats.
3. **Make Repairs**: If Aries' error affected someone, a sincere apology plus an effort to correct the damage can show goodwill.
4. **Move On**: Aries should not dwell too long. Once they have learned and fixed things, it is fine to continue forward. The sign's resilience helps here.

Mistakes can be stepping stones to better methods, boosting Aries' practical experience and emotional maturity.

## 15. Finding Enough Rest

Aries might feel unstoppable but still needs adequate sleep and downtime. Signs that Aries is not resting enough include constant fatigue, irritability, or trouble focusing. Remedies:

- **Set Bedtime Boundaries**: Aries could plan to power down devices at a certain hour, so the mind can shift gears.
- **Active Wind-Down**: Light stretching or a short walk before bed may calm restlessness.
- **Disconnect from Excitement**: If Aries watches intense shows or plays fast-paced games right before sleep, the mind might stay wired. Choosing calmer pre-sleep activities can help.
- **Power Naps**: A quick 15-20 minute nap during the day can recharge an Aries who is consistently on the go.

Adequate rest ensures that Aries' trademark energy is sustainable, reducing mood swings and improving overall health.

## 16. Navigating Over-Competitiveness

Aries is often motivated by beating goals or even friendly competition with others. Yet, when competition turns sour, it can damage friendships or team spirit. To keep it in check:

1. **Set Personal Benchmarks**: Aim to beat last week's score or time, rather than focusing on defeating a specific person.
2. **Cheer Others**: Show sportsmanship by praising a friend's achievement. Aries might say, "Great job! You really improved." This fosters mutual respect.

3. **Avoid Making Everything a Contest**: Not all parts of life need competition. Enjoying a group game for fun can sometimes be more rewarding than pushing to win at all costs.
4. **Notice Negative Feelings**: If Aries feels envy or anger when someone else excels, they can remind themselves that each person's path is unique. This helps shift the mindset from rivalry to personal growth.

Healthy competition can be a spark, but Aries should ensure it remains a positive force, not an obsession that stirs conflict.

## 17. Seeking Advice and Mentorship

Aries often likes being the one in charge, but no one knows everything. By finding mentors or trusted advisors, Aries can skip certain pitfalls. Benefits include:

- **Learning Faster**: Mentors can warn about common errors, helping Aries steer clear of them.
- **Getting Honest Feedback**: Aries might appreciate a mentor who points out areas for improvement, doing so in a supportive way.
- **Expanding Connections**: A mentor can introduce Aries to networks or resources that speed up success.
- **Boosting Confidence**: Knowing an expert is backing them can give Aries a sense of security, making it less risky to explore new fields.

Letting go of the "I must do it alone" mindset can be hard, but the guidance gained often leads to bigger achievements.

## 18. Balancing Self-Confidence with Humility

Aries usually radiates a "can-do" spirit, which is admirable. But if this tilts into arrogance, it can create friction. Tips to strike a balance:

- **Acknowledge Team Efforts**: When a project goes well, Aries can say, "We did great," not just "I did great."
- **Learn from Peers**: Even if Aries is skilled, others have strengths too. Showing genuine interest in others' ideas fosters mutual respect.
- **Admit Knowledge Gaps**: It is fine to say, "I'm not sure about that. Let's find out." This honesty often earns more respect than pretending to know.
- **Compliment Others**: Aries can show appreciation for a friend's skill or coworker's contribution. This reminds everyone that Aries recognizes others' worth.

Being confident yet open-minded allows Aries to shine without overshadowing those around them.

## 19. Addressing Relationship Tensions

In personal relationships—whether romantic, friendship, or family—Aries' direct style can both charm and irritate. If tension arises:

1. **Use Calm Talks**: Aries might set aside a time to discuss issues peacefully, focusing on understanding rather than proving a point.
2. **Respect Boundaries**: Loved ones might need space or a gentler pace. Aries should accept that different personalities have different limits.
3. **Show Warmth**: Aries can remember to do kind gestures, write a short supportive note, or offer help. This balances the moments Aries is intense or demanding.
4. **Apologize Sincerely**: If Aries said something harsh in the heat of the moment, a genuine apology can clear the air.

Healthy relationships involve give and take. Aries can keep passion alive while respecting others' feelings.

# CHAPTER 17: MONEY MATTERS FOR ARIES

Aries is often described as full of bold energy and quick action. This can affect how Aries deals with money—both earning it and spending it. While an Aries might show confidence in their ability to earn, they may also face some struggles with saving or sticking to a plan for the long term. In this chapter, we will focus on how Aries might approach money at home, at work, or in day-to-day life. We will look at how Aries likes to earn, what spending patterns might appear, and how an Aries person can find a balance between being daring and keeping their finances steady. By exploring typical Aries behavior around money, we can find practical tips that fit well with the sign's fiery spirit while also giving them a sense of security.

## 1. Aries and the Drive to Earn

Aries is known for a natural drive. Many Aries folks want to stand on their own feet. They prefer not to wait for others to provide, so they seek ways to earn money. This might show up from a young age: an Aries child may try to sell homemade crafts or set up a lemonade stand. As adults, Aries might enjoy jobs or ventures where pay can grow quickly based on effort. They often prefer roles that reward initiative, such as sales, freelancing, or starting a small business.

- **Direct Action**: Aries does not like beating around the bush. If they want to earn extra money, they will likely leap into action, trying to fix a problem or offer a service. This can be a major plus, as it means they do not procrastinate.

- **Energy and Speed**: An Aries may do well in positions requiring quick decisions or direct results. They might handle short tasks better than slow, drawn-out processes.
- **Risk of Overload**: Because Aries can take on many tasks at once, they risk burnout if they chase too many earning paths simultaneously. Keeping track of time and energy is vital to avoid feeling overwhelmed.

## 2. Impulse vs. Plan in Spending

One of the main financial challenges for Aries can be impulse spending. Aries sees something exciting—a gadget, a course, or a trip—and might spend right away without a second thought. This is tied to the sign's fiery nature, which wants quick rewards. On the other hand, planning requires patience, which Aries might find dull. Balancing impulse and plan can help Aries avoid regret later on.

- **Spotting Impulse Urges**: Aries can train themselves to pause when they want to buy something large or unusual. A simple rule is to wait 24 hours. If the urge remains strong, maybe it is worth it. If it fades, Aries keeps the money.
- **Setting Small Targets**: If Aries wants to buy a big-ticket item, they can break the cost into smaller, manageable goals. Each step can feel like a mini-win, which motivates the sign to save rather than spend right away.
- **Creating a Simple Budget**: A complicated spreadsheet might bore Aries, but a short list of "must-pay" items (rent, bills, groceries) and "fun money" can be enough. Aries can see that once the must-pay items are covered, the rest is free to use, but only up to a certain limit.

# 3. Aries' Earning Style in Different Work Settings

Aries might prefer work setups that let them see results quickly—like commissions in sales or a performance-based bonus in a job. They enjoy direct feedback, especially if higher effort means higher pay. Some Aries folks may do well in competitive roles, pushing themselves to hit targets or beat last month's numbers. However, not every Aries wants a public contest at work. Some prefer to lead a small team or do tasks on their own terms, hoping the payoff grows steadily.

- **Sales and Negotiations**: Aries can excel at pitching ideas if they believe in the product or project. Their direct style might close deals quickly. Still, they must watch out for abrupt speech that may put off sensitive clients.
- **Self-Employed Ventures**: Many Aries enjoy creating their own path, whether it is freelancing, consulting, or running a personal shop. This freedom fits their independent streak. But they must handle the business side carefully, such as tracking invoices or paying taxes on time.
- **Team Jobs with Clear Incentives**: In a corporate setting, if the company rewards quick results, Aries might shine. However, Aries should confirm that the role is not all about waiting for others. If the job is too slow, Aries might grow bored or frustrated.

# 4. Handling Debt and Loans

Because of their willingness to move forward without too much worry, Aries could slip into debt if they are not careful. Maybe they use credit cards for impulsive buys or take a loan to fund a quick opportunity. While a bit of risk can lead to gains, it can also create problems if payments pile up or interest rates climb.

- **Deciding If Debt Is Worth It**: Aries should ask, "Will this debt help me earn more or improve my life in a concrete way?" If the answer is unclear, it might be safer to hold off.
- **Repayment Plan**: If Aries already has debt, they can set a short, clear plan to tackle the balances. Paying off the highest-interest debt first might be wise. Aries might enjoy the sense of victory each time a balance goes down.
- **Avoiding Multiple Loans**: Taking on many loans at once can stress even the boldest Aries. Sticking to one or two manageable debts is usually safer, so Aries can see real progress in paying them off.

## 5. Investing for the Future

Thinking long term can be challenging for Aries, who loves immediate action. Still, smart investing can help Aries build a safety net and open the door to bigger goals. Aries might look for investments that feel lively, such as stocks in companies they support, or even real estate if they like tangible assets. Because Aries might be drawn to high returns, they have to watch for risky schemes or impulsive bets.

- **Learning the Basics**: Even a quick primer on how stocks, bonds, or mutual funds work can guide Aries away from random choices. Aries might read short articles or watch simple videos rather than diving into thick manuals.
- **Setting Short-Term Milestones**: Instead of just a vague "I'll invest for 20 years," Aries can say, "I'll put $X each month into a fund," checking progress quarterly. They can treat each quarter as a mini challenge, seeing how their contribution grows.
- **Balancing Risk**: Aries might get excited by a fast-growing idea, but it is often wise to keep some stable, reliable options

too. This way, if the bold choice flops, there is still a safety net.

## 6. Aries Budgeting Methods

A typical strict budget might frustrate Aries, who does not like being locked into rigid rules. However, a flexible but clear approach can work well:

1. **Divide by Essentials, Fun, and Goals**: Aries can list necessary monthly costs (rent, bills, basic food), a set amount for entertainment or quick choices, and a portion for savings or investing. This keeps it simple.
2. **Use Automatic Transfers**: If Aries sets an auto-transfer to savings right after each paycheck, they can treat that money as off-limits. This is helpful because Aries might not manually save if it requires repeated patience.
3. **Track Just the Big Stuff**: Instead of writing down every single small transaction, Aries might only track large purchases or monthly bills. This lighter approach keeps them aware without feeling trapped by details.
4. **Set a Weekly Cash Limit**: Some Aries do well using physical cash for daily expenses. Once the week's envelope is empty, they wait until the next week. This visual limit can curb random spending.

## 7. Generosity and Giving

Aries can be generous, especially if they see a friend or cause they believe needs help. Their quick reaction might lead them to donate money or buy gifts for others on the spot. While this kindness is admirable, Aries should ensure it does not hinder their own stability. Balancing giving and personal finances is crucial.

- **Plan a Generosity Fund**: Aries might set aside a small budget for helping others or supporting causes each month. Then, if a friend is in need, Aries can dip into that fund without messing up the rest of their plan.
- **Avoid Emotional Traps**: Scams or pushy requests might target Aries' big heart. Before donating a large sum, Aries can confirm the legitimacy of the person or group.
- **Non-Monetary Help**: If the budget is tight, Aries can offer time, skills, or connections instead of cash. Often, Aries' active approach is more valuable than money alone.

## 8. Aries Partnerships and Shared Money

When Aries shares finances with a partner—be it a spouse, sibling, roommate, or friend—some friction can arise because of Aries' direct style. The partner might want to talk decisions through, while Aries may just act. Ensuring both sides feel heard can prevent arguments and lead to better financial outcomes.

- **Agree on Joint Priorities**: If Aries and the partner both want to save for a new place or plan a big event, they can set a shared goal first. This helps Aries see a reason for holding back on smaller impulsive buys.
- **Set Clear Boundaries**: For day-to-day personal spending, each person might keep separate accounts. But for shared bills, they contribute to a joint account. This offers Aries some freedom while still building joint security.
- **Regular Check-Ins**: Meeting once a month for a short money chat can catch any issues early. Aries might prefer a quick, no-nonsense style: "We spent X on groceries, we saved Y for the big goal. Any changes?"
- **Respect Pace Differences**: If the partner is slower or more cautious, Aries can use their own boldness in positive ways, like finding deals or trying new ways to invest. Meanwhile,

the partner can handle detailed tracking. Both roles add value.

## 9. Teaching Aries Children About Money

If a young Aries is in the family, teaching them about money early can shape healthy habits. Aries kids might show strong will, so making it fun and interactive helps. They often like tasks with quick results:

- **Small Allowance for Tasks**: Give them simple chores with a small payment. Aries can learn that effort leads to earnings. They might save up for a toy, feeling proud of each coin.
- **Short Savings Goals**: A younger Aries might lose interest if the goal is too far away. Let them pick something they want in a few weeks or a couple of months at most.
- **Games and Challenges**: Simple board games or mobile apps that teach basic money lessons can keep Aries engaged. They might enjoy "who can save the most in a month" if they see it as a friendly contest.
- **Encourage Generosity**: Aries children can also learn to share a part of their allowance with a cause or a small gift. This teaches them that giving is part of dealing with money, not just spending on themselves.

## 10. Negotiating Salary or Pay

Because Aries is direct, they might be good at asking for a raise or a better deal, but they should plan carefully. Aries sometimes rushes or uses overly forceful words, which can backfire. Instead, a thoughtful approach can yield better pay:

1. **Know the Value**: Aries can list reasons why they deserve higher pay, such as recent achievements or how they help the company grow.

2. **Practice Calm Delivery**: Aries might rehearse a polite but firm way of speaking, ensuring they do not sound aggressive.
3. **Timing**: Aries should pick a time when the boss or client is open to talk, maybe after a project success. Barging in during a busy, stressful moment can harm the request.
4. **Use Clear Numbers**: Instead of vague statements, Aries might say, "Based on my added duties, I believe a salary of X is fair." Clarity often works better than broad demands.

With the right blend of confidence and respect, Aries can secure pay raises that match their strong work ethic.

## 11. Aries Entrepreneurs and Start-Ups

Many Aries folks dream of starting a company or running a side hustle. Their quick energy is great for launching things. Yet they should keep an eye on details like cost control, legal rules, and marketing approaches:

- **Action-Oriented Launch**: Aries can run a small test version of a product or service. They do not have to wait for perfect conditions. This early start can give them feedback to refine the offer.
- **Managing Expenses**: Aries might get excited about fancy office setups or extra tools. A basic approach can save money in the early stage. Aries can expand once profit is steady.
- **Delegation**: Handling every job alone can exhaust Aries. Finding a partner or hiring someone with careful planning skills can balance Aries' enthusiasm.
- **Staying Organized**: Even if Aries dislikes daily records, a simple system for tracking sales, costs, and deadlines is crucial. Setting aside a small time each week for paperwork can prevent chaos.

When Aries combines creativity with basic financial sense, their business can flourish and stand out in the market.

## 12. Avoiding Scams and Get-Rich-Quick Offers

Aries might be a prime target for flashy promises, because they love fast progress and direct success. Scammers might lure Aries with phrases like "Huge returns in a short time!" or "Act now, or lose out!" Aries should be cautious:

1. **Research First**: If a proposal sounds too good to be true, Aries can do a quick search or ask a trusted advisor. Scammy offers often crumble under scrutiny.
2. **Take Time**: A real opportunity will let Aries think or consult others. Pressure to act instantly is a red flag.
3. **Check Credentials**: Aries can look for reviews, official licenses, or a history of the group's track record. If details are lacking, it might be safer to walk away.
4. **Listen to Gut Feel**: Aries often has strong instincts. If they sense something off, or if the pitch feels pushy, stepping back is wise.

Protecting money is just as important as making it, and Aries can learn that not every exciting pitch is worth the risk.

## 13. Building a Savings Cushion

Even if Aries wants to invest in big ideas, having an emergency fund can calm everyday worries. Aries might prefer a simpler approach to saving, rather than complex rules:

- **Auto-Deposit**: By sending a small amount to a separate savings account each payday, Aries can slowly gather a cushion without manual effort.

- **Naming the Account**: If Aries calls it something motivational (like "Security Fund" or "Freedom Pot"), they might be less tempted to dip into it for random buys.
- **Small Goals**: For example, Aries can try to save one month's living costs first. Once that is reached, aim for two months, and so on. Each step can feel like a quick success.
- **Use a Suitable Format**: Aries might keep the emergency fund in a simple savings account rather than locking it away. That way, it is accessible when truly needed, but it also stays somewhat out of sight daily.

Having even a basic savings buffer can let Aries take bold steps without the fear that one setback will ruin their finances.

## 14. Handling Unexpected Expenses

Cars break down, medical bills appear, or home repairs pop up. Because Aries is used to charging forward, an unplanned bill can be frustrating. Yet, with a bit of strategy:

- **Emergency Funds**: As mentioned, having some money saved is the first line of defense. Aries can pay the urgent cost and keep going.
- **Negotiation Skills**: Aries can try negotiating with the service provider. Sometimes, they can arrange a payment plan or get a small discount if they pay quickly.
- **Prioritize**: If Aries faces multiple unexpected costs, they must decide which is most urgent. Fixing a car for daily transport might come before fixing a small home detail.
- **Stay Calm**: When Aries sees an unwelcome bill, they might burst into annoyance. Taking a deep breath and focusing on solutions helps them tackle the problem rather than stew in frustration.

Aries can handle surprises better if they have a calm plan. This also preserves their lively energy for more positive uses.

## 15. Aries' Mindset on Risk and Reward

Aries is not afraid to take a chance, especially if a reward seems big or exciting. This can be a double-edged sword. While some risk can lead to success, too much risk can drain money or create stress. To manage risk wisely:

- **Assess the Worst Case**: Aries can ask themselves, "What is the worst outcome if this fails?" If the answer is losing all the money needed for rent, the risk may be too high.
- **Set Risk Limits**: Aries might decide on a maximum amount they are willing to put at risk—maybe 5-10% of their savings. This ensures the rest stays safe.
- **Research, Then Act**: Being bold does not mean skipping homework. Even a few hours spent understanding the potential pitfalls can save Aries from big losses.
- **Plan for Ups and Downs**: If Aries invests in something volatile, they should brace themselves for changes in value or delays. Emotional ups and downs can be managed better if expected.

By staying within reason, Aries can keep the thrill of bold moves without risking total financial chaos.

## 16. Aries' Public Style with Money

Some Aries folks like showing success—perhaps upgrading a car, wearing nice outfits, or hosting friends in a bright, stylish home. While there is nothing wrong with enjoying the fruits of one's labor, Aries should be sure it aligns with their true budget and not just an image.

- **Personal Values vs. Image**: Aries can ask, "Am I buying this to impress others, or because I truly value it?" This question keeps them honest.
- **Avoid Overspending for Show**: If Aries is not actually able to afford certain luxuries, the short-term boost in pride may lead to long-term stress.
- **Use Confidence Wisely**: Aries does not need fancy items to appear strong. Their natural spark is enough to leave a memorable impression.
- **Treats vs. Lifestyle**: An occasional treat for oneself is fine, but turning those treats into a daily habit can blow a budget quickly.

Balancing the desire to stand out with healthy money choices helps Aries enjoy life without running into hidden problems later.

## 17. Overcoming Slumps or Financial Mistakes

Aries might at times make a sudden decision that leads to a loss—maybe a rushed investment or a big purchase they regret. Dwelling on errors can bring negative feelings. Instead, Aries can:

1. **Accept the Loss**: Once it is done, it is done. Aries can channel regret into learning.
2. **Review Mistakes**: Pinpoint which step was flawed (lack of research, impulsive buy, ignoring advice?). Next time, Aries can watch for that pattern.
3. **Create a Recovery Plan**: If the mistake caused debt, set a repayment approach. If it drained savings, focus on rebuilding a portion each month.
4. **Move Forward**: Aries thrives on action. By taking steps to fix the error, they regain confidence. Holding onto guilt might freeze them.

Mistakes do not define an Aries. The sign's resilience can transform mishaps into valuable lessons that make future decisions smarter and stronger.

## 18. Family and Money Traditions

Some Aries people grow up in families with strong money traditions—maybe saving for big events or being taught to spend carefully. Others might come from families that rarely discuss money. Aries can shape their own path, but it helps to reflect on what they learned (or did not learn) at home:

- **Keeping Helpful Habits**: If the family taught a good system for saving or budgeting, Aries might adopt a simpler version that suits their energetic style.
- **Dropping Unhelpful Patterns**: If Aries saw money used in a controlling or reckless way at home, they can decide to break that cycle by learning new behaviors.
- **Open Talks**: Aries might speak with parents or siblings about what worked and what did not. Hearing different perspectives can spark new ideas.
- **Creating Personal Traditions**: Aries can form positive money habits in their household—like a weekly chat about expenses or a quick plan for the next financial step. This fosters a supportive environment.

Thinking about family background can give Aries insight into hidden beliefs about money, which they can modify as needed for a better present and future.

## 19. Tracking Progress Over Time

Aries may not love elaborate spreadsheets, but checking financial growth can be motivating if done in a straightforward way:

- **Quarterly Snapshots**: Every three months, Aries can note how much they have in savings, how much debt remains, and any new investments. They might record these numbers in a small notebook or a simple app.
- **Celebrate Key Milestones**: If debt shrinks by half, or savings hits a nice round figure, Aries can mark the moment with a small reward or a happy announcement to close friends.
- **Visual Charts**: Aries might put a small chart on the fridge or in a private folder, seeing how the line goes up or down over time. This visual can push them to keep going.
- **Adjusting Goals**: If progress is faster or slower than expected, Aries can adjust the plan. That might mean adding more each month to savings or paying down debt at a different pace.

Such a routine does not need to be tedious. Aries can keep it short and dynamic. Noticing real progress can fuel their sense of accomplishment.

# CHAPTER 18: ARIES & THEIR PUBLIC IMAGE

Aries is often seen as the "spark" of the zodiac, someone ready to lead or charge ahead. Because of this, people may notice Aries right away in social settings or in public roles. But how does Aries' natural style affect how others view them? In this chapter, we will explore how Aries might appear to friends, colleagues, or strangers, and how Aries can handle issues that arise from public perception. We will look at how Aries may project confidence, how to handle misunderstandings, and ways to stay true to their fiery nature without coming across as overbearing. By understanding how their public image forms, Aries can shape it in a way that reflects their best qualities.

## 1. First Impressions: Bold and Direct

Aries tends to make a strong impression on first meeting. The sign is known for speaking openly, standing with a confident stance, and taking initiative in group situations. This can lead people to see Aries as a natural leader or someone who does not shy away from being in the spotlight.

- **Pros**: Many appreciate Aries for being honest and active right from the start. In group events, Aries might be the one to say, "Let's get started!" or "Here's an idea." This directness can be refreshing.
- **Cons**: Some might feel overshadowed or think Aries is too pushy if they wanted a slower pace or a quieter introduction. This risk is higher if Aries forgets to listen before jumping in.

- **Tip**: Aries can balance their bright entrance by showing warmth to others, asking them a short question about themselves, or offering a quick compliment to lighten the mood.

## 2. Aries on Social Media and Online Presence

In today's world, public image often includes how we present ourselves online. Aries may use social platforms to share achievements or opinions. This can be positive—Aries might post exciting updates that spark interest—but there are pitfalls.

- **Bold Updates**: Aries might post strong views or major news about their projects. This can attract likes or comments, but also might stir debate if the topic is sensitive.
- **Fast Reactions**: If someone leaves a rude comment, Aries might fire back quickly. A calmer approach or ignoring trolls often avoids drama.
- **Showing Authentic Energy**: The best online style for Aries is genuine. They might share quick snippets of daily life, new ideas, or fun photos. People who follow Aries appreciate that direct, upbeat tone.
- **Over-Posting**: Aries might get carried away and post multiple times a day about every small milestone. Moderation can keep the feed interesting without overwhelming followers.

## 3. Standing Out in Groups

Aries usually does not like to fade into the background. Whether it is a work meeting, a community gathering, or a party, Aries might step forward with suggestions or lead the conversation. This can build a public image of someone who is confident and unafraid to take charge.

- **Positive Outcomes**: People who want direction might depend on Aries to move things along. Aries' strong presence can prevent a group from stalling.
- **Possible Problems**: Others with leadership ambitions or quieter personalities might resent Aries if they always grab the spotlight. Aries can avoid friction by asking, "Anyone else want to add something?"
- **Building Goodwill**: Aries can share the stage, letting others speak or lead certain parts of a project. This generosity in letting others shine can make Aries appear more caring and respectful.

## 4. Aries in Professional Settings

At work, Aries might quickly earn a reputation as someone who takes on big tasks without fear. Supervisors may appreciate Aries' direct manner. However, coworkers might be cautious if Aries seems to push them aside or if Aries demands action too fast.

- **Earning Respect**: Aries should back up confidence with real effort. If they volunteer for a project, they need to follow through so others see that energy put to good use.
- **Handling Competition**: Aries might clash with coworkers who also want recognition. A wise Aries can keep competition friendly, praising teammates while highlighting their own successes calmly.
- **Presentation and Meetings**: If Aries leads a meeting, they might speak in a clear, direct style, which can be well-received. They just have to ensure they do not dismiss questions or skip over details that others need.

## 5. How Strangers Often View Aries

Strangers or acquaintances might notice Aries as lively, straightforward, and maybe even "brave." Aries often moves with purpose—like striding into a store confidently or speaking up at a local event. However, not everyone responds well to strong personalities, especially if they expect quiet courtesy.

- **Friendly and Open**: If Aries greets people with a smile and direct eye contact, the first impression is often positive. People might call Aries "someone who seems sure of themselves."
- **Risk of Misreading**: Some strangers might think Aries is arrogant if the sign forgets to show polite interest in them. Asking a short, sincere question about the other person's day or opinion can balance Aries' self-assured vibe.
- **Moments of Conflict**: In any dispute with strangers (like a line at the store, a parking issue, or a short disagreement in public), Aries might respond passionately. Others could be taken aback. Calmer words can reduce tension.

## 6. Aries Image with Friends and Family

Close friends and family know the deeper side of Aries. They see not just the bold exterior but also the warm heart or the times Aries might feel unsure. Still, Aries' public image among loved ones might be shaped by how they handle group events, conflicts, or celebrations.

- **The "Protector" Role**: Aries might stand up for siblings or friends, defending them in tough spots. This can earn respect and gratitude.
- **Potential "Bossiness"**: Sometimes Aries tries to direct family plans without asking if everyone agrees. Over time, relatives

might label them as bossy. A quick check-in—"Should we do it this way?"—fixes that.
- **Fun and Surprises**: Aries might throw spontaneous get-togethers or plan surprising outings. This can build a lively image. Loved ones may call Aries the "spark plug" of the family, always ready for action.

## 7. Aries and Public Speaking

Aries often does well if they choose to speak in public—like giving a presentation, leading a workshop, or simply sharing a short talk at a local event. Their direct style can keep people's attention. A few points to ensure success:

- **Structure**: Aries should outline main points beforehand. Rushing in without a basic plan might lead to rambling.
- **Energy**: Using a confident tone and natural gestures can show Aries' passion. The audience often responds to honest enthusiasm.
- **Listening for Feedback**: If it is a workshop or interactive session, Aries should pause to let others ask questions or share thoughts. This keeps the talk from feeling like a one-way lecture.
- **Ending Strong**: Aries might wrap up with a clear, concise statement. That final punch can leave the audience feeling energized.

## 8. Handling Rumors or Negative Perceptions

Because Aries is visible and direct, they might attract gossip if some folks misunderstand their motives. Perhaps someone calls them "too intense" or "arrogant." Aries can address this calmly:

- **Evaluate the Source**: If the rumor comes from a minor or jealous source, Aries might ignore it. If it is harming important relationships, Aries might clear things up.
- **Set the Record Straight**: Aries can talk privately to the person spreading negativity, explaining their side. A calm talk can solve many problems.
- **Show True Intent**: Actions speak louder than words. If Aries was labeled "uncaring," they might show consistent kindness in group efforts, letting the truth replace gossip.
- **Avoid Overreaction**: Aries might want to snap at gossip, but that could worsen the situation. A balanced approach—firm but polite—often works better.

## 9. Aries and Public Positions of Leadership

If Aries moves into a bigger public role—like managing a large team or running for local office—people will watch closely. Aries can use their fearless spark to inspire others, but should also keep these points in mind:

1. **Transparency**: Being open about goals and decisions fosters trust. Aries can do short updates about progress, so people do not feel left in the dark.
2. **Respecting Different Views**: In a broad public role, many viewpoints appear. Aries cannot please everyone by charging ahead with a single vision. Listening sessions or Q&A events can help Aries connect with diverse groups.
3. **Staying Professional**: Aries' temper might flare if faced with criticism. But in a public role, a calm, reasoned reply is needed to maintain a solid image.
4. **Delegation**: Aries should not try to handle every detail alone. Letting others contribute fosters a team spirit, reducing the chance of Aries being seen as controlling.

## 10. Presenting Oneself in Media or Interviews

If Aries is interviewed—maybe on TV, a podcast, or even for a local newspaper—how do they ensure a positive, accurate image? Because Aries can speak quickly and with strong feelings, planning a bit is wise:

- **Key Messages**: Aries might list the top three points they want to share, ensuring they do not stray off topic.
- **Concise Answers**: Keeping statements short and direct helps the interviewer and audience understand. Aries' natural clarity can shine here.
- **Calm Tone Under Pressure**: If asked a tough question, Aries can pause briefly before replying, staying polite. Rushing to respond might lead to confusing or defensive words.
- **Eye Contact and Body Language**: A confident posture, looking at the interviewer (or camera), and a friendly expression match Aries' usual style. Just avoid fidgeting or crossing arms, which might appear tense.

## 11. Managing a Reputation for Impatience

Aries often faces jokes or comments like, "They can't wait for anything." In public, if Aries shows impatience too often, it might overshadow their positive qualities. To handle this:

- **Patience "Micro-Goals"**: For instance, Aries can decide, "I will wait an extra minute before offering my view," or "I will let two others speak first in a meeting."
- **Visual Reminders**: Aries could keep a simple reminder on their phone or desk: "Pause. Listen." This can prevent reflex action.
- **Humor**: Sometimes, Aries can joke about their own impatience in a light-hearted way. This shows self-awareness and can make others feel more at ease.

- **Celebrate Calm Moments**: If Aries handles a situation calmly, they can acknowledge that success internally. Over time, the label of "always impatient" might fade as people see the new behavior.

## 12. Shifting from "Me" to "Us"

Because Aries is so action-focused, they may unintentionally draw attention to themselves: "I did this," "I decided that." Even if it is true, this might appear self-centered in public. Balancing "me" talk with "us" talk helps:

- **Credit Others**: If a team project succeeds, Aries can say, "We worked together and achieved this." This not only feels fair but also shows Aries can share the spotlight.
- **Ask for Input**: In public, Aries might say, "I have a plan, but I want to hear your ideas." This approach can build an image of a cooperative leader.
- **Use Inclusive Language**: Phrases like "Our community" or "Our group" remind people that Aries is thinking beyond personal gain.

## 13. Aries and Community Involvement

Many Aries want to bring change or do something active in their local community. Leading a neighborhood project, coaching a kids' sports team, or volunteering can shape Aries' public image in a positive way. Still, there are a few tips:

- **Set Clear Goals**: If Aries heads a community drive, they might define a specific outcome: "We'll clean this park within two weekends." Clarity helps volunteers know what to do.
- **Stay Organized**: Aries can become excited about big ideas but might skip the follow-up steps. Having a simple checklist

or a co-organizer with a detail-oriented style ensures tasks are done.
- **Celebrate Group Wins**: If the community success is reached, Aries can share the credit widely. This fosters goodwill.
- **Balance Speed with Inclusion**: Aries might want to act right away, but involving others in the planning can make them feel valued. That leads to stronger support.

## 14. Turning Down the Volume When Needed

In some public spaces—like a quiet meeting, a solemn event, or a library—Aries might accidentally speak too loudly or act too boldly. This can harm their image among those who expect calm. Strategies for quiet influence:

- **Read the Room**: Aries can observe how others behave. If people speak softly, Aries can match that volume. If many are taking turns to talk, Aries can wait for a proper opening.
- **Gentle Expressions**: Instead of jumping to the front, Aries might ask politely if they can contribute or step forward. This subtle approach can surprise those who expect Aries to be loud all the time.
- **Find Other Outlets**: If Aries needs to vent energy, they might take a short break outside, do a mental puzzle, or write notes. Then, they can return calmly.

## 15. Cultural Differences

Aries who travels or works in diverse environments might find that some cultures value open, direct talk, while others see it as rude. Being aware of local customs helps Aries avoid negative misunderstandings:

- **Observe Before Acting**: Aries can watch how locals greet each other or make decisions. If the norm is slower discussions, Aries can slow down.
- **Ask for Guidance**: A friendly local or colleague can share tips on what is acceptable. Aries' willingness to adapt shows respect.
- **Maintain Authenticity**: Adapting does not mean Aries must hide their core personality. It is more about small adjustments, like speaking more gently or waiting for senior members to speak first.
- **Embrace Patience**: In a place that values indirect communication, Aries might find it tricky. However, learning a bit of patience can keep Aries from clashing with local norms.

## 16. Aries and Public Conflict

Sometimes, Aries may face open disagreement or confrontations in front of others. Because Aries can respond with strong emotion, they need a plan:

- **Stay Composed**: Taking a deep breath or counting to five can help Aries speak calmly. Yelling in public might harm the sign's image.
- **Use Simple Explanations**: Aries can say, "I see your point, but I disagree because..." Then, briefly clarify. This direct but polite style suits Aries' nature while showing respect.
- **Offer Solutions**: Instead of focusing on the argument, Aries can shift to possible fixes. This shows leadership and maturity.
- **Know When to End**: If the dispute is going nowhere, Aries might suggest moving the talk offline or in private. This avoids a public scene.

## 17. Aries' Effect on Their Circle

Friends often mention that being around Aries gives them energy—like they are charged up by Aries' enthusiasm. But a friend might also say, "Aries can be hard to keep up with." By finding a steady rhythm, Aries can avoid wearing out the people they care about.

- **Check for Signs of Overwhelm**: If friends seem tired or start to say "I need a break," Aries can tone down the pace.
- **Plan Calm Hangouts Too**: Not every meet-up has to be an extreme adventure. Sometimes, a low-key dinner or quiet board game night helps everyone relax.
- **Invite Input**: Aries can ask, "What do you want to do?" This ensures friends or family do not feel they always have to follow Aries' fast lead.
- **Be the Cheerleader**: Aries' public image can improve further if they cheer on their friends' achievements. This shows that Aries is not only about their own spotlight but also supporting others.

## 18. Dealing with Stage Fright or Self-Doubt

Surprisingly, some Aries folks feel nervous before stepping into the public eye, even though they appear brave. They might worry about failing or being judged. Handling this:

1. **Small Practice**: Aries can rehearse in front of a mirror or a friend, channeling that fiery energy into prepared lines or steps.
2. **Positive Self-Talk**: Aries might remind themselves, "I've got this. I am prepared. I've done hard things before." This direct approach can quiet doubts.

3. **Focus on the Action**: Instead of thinking, "Everyone is watching me," Aries can think, "I'm here to share something helpful." Shifting focus to the task can ease tension.
4. **Use the Rush**: The same adrenaline that causes nerves can be harnessed for a lively performance. Once Aries starts, they may find that their natural spark takes over.

## 19. Keeping a Balanced Image Over Time

Aries might enjoy the thrill of short bursts—like leading one big event or stepping up for a short project. But a public image also forms over the long run. Consistency matters:

- **Stable Reliability**: Aries can build trust by consistently following through on promises. If they vow to show up at 9, they do. If they agree to finish a job by Friday, it is done. Over time, this reliability strengthens their public image.
- **Adapting as They Grow**: People might expect Aries to always be the same. But as Aries matures, they can keep the bright energy while adding patience and calmness. Letting others see that growth can impress them.
- **Handling Tiring Seasons**: If Aries is in a busy phase, they may not be able to maintain the same pace publicly. Being honest—"I'm taking a step back for a bit"—is better than disappearing without explanation.

# CHAPTER 19: ARIES ACROSS DIFFERENT STAGES OF LIFE

Aries energy does not remain static. It can express itself in distinct ways as a person grows older and encounters new experiences. In earlier chapters, we looked at Aries as children, teens, and adults, but here we will examine, in one place, how Aries might change from early life to later years. We will focus on each life stage, asking how typical Aries traits—like boldness, quickness, enthusiasm, and directness—may show themselves during that period. By seeing Aries in all phases, we can gain insight into how this sign's spark can brighten a lifetime when handled well.

## 1. Infancy and Toddler Years: An Eager Start

**Early Signs of Fire**

Many parents of Aries infants say their babies show strong reactions early. This can appear as a loud cry when hungry or an intense squeal of joy when happy. Aries' directness can shine through even before they speak: they might reach out boldly for objects, roll over fast, or try to crawl or walk earlier than expected.

**Toddler Exploration**

Once they can move, Aries toddlers often roam around without fear. They might be the first among their playmates to climb a small slide or open a cabinet to see what is inside. This boldness can be fun to watch, but parents must be extra cautious about safety measures because Aries toddlers might not sense danger as readily.

**Emotional Bumps**

When upset, Aries toddlers can have short but intense tantrums. At this age, they do not yet know how to handle big feelings calmly. Simple methods, such as redirecting their attention or giving them a quick physical activity, can help them settle. Patience from parents is vital, as Aries children respond well to calm but firm guidance rather than harsh scolding.

**Tips for Parents**

- Provide safe ways to explore, like soft play areas or a well-guarded backyard.
- Encourage early attempts at new skills, but supervise closely.
- Use clear, consistent rules; Aries toddlers might test limits often.
- Show excitement for their efforts. This builds confidence in a small but direct child.

## 2. Childhood (Ages 4–10): Expanding Curiosity

**Eager to Learn**
In school or at home, Aries children often dive into new activities with zeal. They may raise their hands first in class, even if they do not know the full answer. They enjoy being recognized, so teachers and parents can harness this by praising honest attempts. Aries children might also enjoy group projects if given a chance to take the lead, but they must learn to share roles with peers.

**Active Play**
Aries kids usually thrive on active play—sports, racing games, or backyard adventures. They might gather friends for quick matches or short challenges. Group sports can teach them teamwork and the value of patience when others move at a slower pace. If Aries kids dislike slow tasks like puzzles or reading long passages, parents can break such tasks into small chunks or mix them with physical breaks.

### Emotional Growth

As Aries children enter middle childhood, they start understanding their feelings a bit better. However, they can still lose patience quickly. Teaching simple calming methods—like counting to five or taking a short walk—helps them manage frustration. They might also need reminders to consider others' feelings. Aries' direct speech can hurt more sensitive friends if not guided toward kindness.

### Tips for Caregivers and Teachers

- Engage them in group sports or drama clubs where they can channel energy positively.
- Introduce brief chores at home to instill responsibility.
- Encourage polite listening: "Let your friend finish talking first."
- Reward progress with small, direct praise (e.g., "Great job finishing your reading!").

## 3. Early Teens (Ages 11–14): Testing Independence

### Surge of Self-Expression

When entering the teen phase, Aries might assert themselves more strongly. They could question rules, challenge authority, and seek more control over daily life. This can lead to clashes at home or school if they feel stifled. However, if given structured freedom—like choosing which extracurricular activities they want—they can thrive.

### Social Circles

Aries teens often like to be around peers who share their active spirit. They might form quick friendships with those who appreciate bold ideas or a fast pace. Yet, if their circle includes quieter friends, Aries teens must be guided to respect different personalities. Some Aries teens can turn overly competitive, especially in sports or academics, so gentle reminders about fair play and empathy matter.

### Curiosity About Identity

As with many teens, Aries might experiment with personal style or new interests. They could shift from one hobby to another. This exploration is normal. Instead of scolding them for changing paths, parents can help them set mini-goals within each interest so the teen sees real achievement before switching. Aries thrives on quick feedback, so they might leave an activity if it feels too slow or uncertain.

### Family Harmony

Conflicts can spark if Aries teens feel restricted. Open conversations—"Why do we have this rule?"—can help them understand reasons behind guidelines. Teaching them negotiation skills allows them to voice opinions without shouting. When Aries teens are heard, they tend to respond with more cooperation.

## 4. Late Teens (Ages 15–18): Shaping Future Choices

### Rising Ambitions

Aries often begins forging an adult path at this stage, thinking about higher education or work. They may have big dreams—leading a sports team, performing in a play, or launching a small project. Their enthusiasm can be an asset if directed properly. However, they might aim too high too fast, ignoring practical steps. Mentors can guide them to set short-term goals on the way to big aims.

### Peer Influence

Aries teens may hold firm to personal viewpoints, making them less swayed by peer pressure in some areas. Yet they might still jump into risky behaviors if they see it as a thrilling test or a quick chance at excitement. Clear talks about consequences can help. Aries benefits from honest discussions that treat them as smart enough to handle real facts.

### Preparing for Independence
They might want to drive early, earn money, or move out soon. If they prove responsible—managing school tasks or part-time jobs—giving them increasing freedom can build confidence. Aries might do well in a job where quick results are noticed, like sales or a small hustle. They learn real-world lessons by facing immediate feedback on performance.

### Family Relationships
Near adulthood, Aries might push for more space. Parents can remain supportive by respecting that space but staying available when Aries needs help. If rules feel fair and well-explained, Aries is less likely to rebel out of frustration.

## 5. Early Adulthood (Ages 19–29): Launching into the World

### Personal Identity Growth
Young Aries often enters this phase eager to prove themselves. They might choose active careers, start small businesses, or travel for fresh experiences. While they love the thrill of new settings, they may need guidance on balancing quick moves with careful steps—like building a stable financial base or finishing training programs before leaping to the next thing.

### Social Circles and Dating
Aries might explore deeper bonds. Some may have short relationships if the initial spark fades. Over time, they learn that not everything can stay at maximum excitement. A partner who balances Aries by offering calm moments might help them see the beauty of steady support. Aries can remain direct in love, which is appealing for those who appreciate honesty.

### Work and Goals
Many Aries in their twenties chase goals with passion. They might

excel in roles that reward action—like marketing, event planning, or management of small teams. However, they must watch for burnout from saying "yes" to every project. Learning to manage daily tasks and plan for the future is a lesson of this stage. Once Aries masters time and energy, they can shoot forward quickly.

**Living Arrangements**
Aries might want their own place as soon as they can afford it, valuing independence. They may decorate in a bold style, with bright colors or modern touches. This desire for personal space is a reflection of Aries wanting to do things on their own terms. Shared housing can work if housemates respect Aries' need to act freely, but open communication about chores or bills helps avoid clashes.

## 6. The 30s and 40s: Maturing Without Losing Spark

**Career and Family**
Aries might find a solid footing around their 30s, having tested various jobs or paths. By now, they likely know which activities keep them energized. If they settle into a profession, they may rise into leadership roles, fueled by confidence and direct communication. Some Aries might balance this with family life, where they bring a playful spirit to the household.

**Deepening Relationships**
If Aries decides on a long-term bond, they can learn to share decisions, practicing patience and empathy. They might value a partner who respects their direct style but also knows how to calmly slow them down when needed. Friendships can also mature, shifting from purely fun-based gatherings to more meaningful support. Aries can still lead friend groups to do exciting outings, but now with a bit more planning.

**Handling Responsibilities**
Mortgages, career commitments, children's schedules—these can

feel restricting to an Aries spirit that loves spontaneity. Yet Aries can adapt by viewing these tasks as challenges to tackle. "I'll handle the bills by Monday," or "I'll plan a short family outing that fits our budget." By framing responsibilities as goals with visible outcomes, Aries can keep that "can-do" attitude.

### Maintaining Personal Projects
Aries might still long for side projects or creative outlets. Hobbies like painting, writing, or short sports leagues can keep life fresh. Aries should avoid letting daily tasks consume all energy. Balancing routine with personal excitement can keep Aries thriving through mid-life.

## 7. The 50s and 60s: A Blend of Experience and Passion

### Career Transitions
Some Aries might stay in a stable job they love, using their experience to mentor younger colleagues. Others might pivot to a brand-new field if they feel bored. Aries' drive to see new frontiers does not fade with age, though they might weigh risks more carefully now.

### Family and Social Roles
If Aries has grown children, they might focus on guiding them gently—though they must watch for being overly direct or pushy. Grandchildren (if present) can see Aries as a playful figure who plans mini-adventures. Aries might also step into community roles, like organizing local clubs or events, where their strong presence is welcomed.

### Health and Activity
Aries may remain active if they have kept up with exercise or chosen sports throughout adult life. Still, they might notice changes in stamina or joint comfort. Adjusting workouts to lower impact activities—like swimming or brisk walks—can help maintain strength.

Aries can turn these routines into friendly challenges to stay motivated.

**Emotional Maturity**
 By this stage, Aries hopefully has learned from earlier mistakes around impatience or short tempers. They can channel passion into constructive talks, showing warmth and fairness. People around them might see a calmer but still bright spark. Aries can inspire others to keep living with excitement at every age.

## 8. The 70s and Beyond: Cherishing Vital Spark

**Refining Priorities**
 In later years, Aries might decide to focus on what truly matters, whether that is family, a passion project, or volunteer work. The sign may no longer want to chase every opportunity. Instead, Aries picks a few interests that bring true satisfaction. They can still be bold in those chosen areas, leading small groups of peers in local causes or creative clubs.

**Staying Connected**
 Aries in older age might enjoy social events where they can share stories of their bold past exploits—career highlights, travel tales, or big achievements. Younger folks might see Aries as an example of living life with spirit. However, Aries may also need to adapt to slower pace gatherings or family visits, being patient if grandchildren or relatives have calmer ways.

**Health Considerations**
 If Aries keeps a bit of daily movement—stretches, short walks, or light classes—they can maintain energy. A healthy diet and regular check-ups can prevent bigger problems. Aries might initially resist the idea of slowing down, but a mindful approach helps them remain active for longer. They can still show that Aries spark by planning day trips or group outings suited to their physical ability.

### Sharing Wisdom

Over decades, Aries gathers stories of acting swiftly, taking risks, and handling outcomes. Passing on these lessons to younger friends or family can be a positive legacy. Aries might do this through casual chats, writing short memoirs, or mentoring youth in the community. Their direct approach, honed by experience, can guide others to be brave but also balanced.

## 9. Common Shifts and Lessons at Each Stage

### Growing in Patience

From a toddler's tantrums to a senior's calm advice, Aries learns gradually that not everything can be forced or rushed. Each life stage presents situations where Aries must wait, whether for a teacher's instructions, a business partner's decisions, or a grandchild's slower walk. Through these moments, Aries develops patience and empathy.

### Learning to Share Spotlight

In childhood, Aries might hog attention. In teen years, they might notice friction if they overshadow classmates. By adulthood, they see that teamwork demands hearing other voices. Many Aries discover that letting others shine does not dim their own light; it often enhances group success.

### Accepting Guidance and Giving It

Younger Aries might resist rules or advice. Later, they realize mentors can accelerate progress. By middle age or beyond, some Aries become mentors themselves, blending directness with warmth. They remember what it felt like to be eager and new, so they pass on practical tips to the next generation.

### Maintaining a Spirit of Action

Regardless of age, Aries usually keeps a certain readiness to "do." They do not want to sit idle for long. Whether it is choosing a new craft in retirement, organizing a block party in mid-life, or taking a leadership role in teen clubs, the thread of Aries is always movement and excitement. Over time, they learn to channel that spark in ways that build stable outcomes rather than short fizzles.

## 10. Across Life's Challenges

### Periods of Change
Major changes—like moving cities, switching careers, divorce, health shifts, or losses—can test Aries. Their natural strategy might be to handle problems head-on, sometimes taking bold steps that others see as impulsive. While this can solve issues quickly, Aries also benefits from pausing to plan, getting advice, and checking emotional well-being.

### Managing Setbacks
Aries might handle smaller setbacks with a shrug: "Oh well, let's try a different path." But bigger failures or personal disappointments can shake them. Learning to open up, possibly seeking support from friends, family, or counselors, can help Aries bounce back stronger. Over a lifetime, Aries may refine the art of resilience, knowing that each setback is a step toward deeper wisdom.

### Health and Self-Care
Because Aries invests energy in many endeavors, they must remain aware of signs of burnout, fatigue, or ignoring minor health issues. Each life stage calls for slightly different health routines. Younger Aries might do intense sports, while older Aries may prefer moderate exercises. Regular check-ups, balanced meals, and stress management are essential to keep that spark bright.

### Emotional Evolution
When younger, Aries might be prone to outbursts or a sense of "Me first!" With age, they can learn calm sharing of feelings. They may discover that vulnerability builds stronger bonds. By older

adulthood, Aries might be a role model for how to express passion without causing harm. Their emotional evolution is one of the most rewarding arcs of Aries life.

## 11. Embracing Fresh Starts at Every Age

### Passion for New Beginnings
Throughout life, Aries often feels drawn to begin fresh. It might be a new job, a new hobby, a new relationship, or a new volunteer position. Some people fear change, but Aries tends to see it as an opportunity to do something exciting. Even in later years, they might pick up an unfamiliar craft or explore a cause they never tried before.

### Handling Others' Reactions
Friends or family might get concerned if Aries changes direction too often. They might worry Aries is unstable or never satisfied. Aries can reassure them that trying new paths is part of staying engaged. Still, Aries should show that they make these changes thoughtfully, not just out of restlessness. Letting loved ones see a plan or reason behind the shift can ease worries.

### Growing Through Reinvention
Aries people often thrive when they can reinvent themselves. Each reinvention does not erase the past but builds upon it. By middle or older age, an Aries might have multiple careers or skill sets. They can look back and see how each stage enriched their perspective.

## 12. Community Legacy

### Leading Projects
Aries who remain active in local groups—whether children's sports leagues, neighborhood initiatives, or civic boards—can leave a lasting mark. The sign's direct style keeps tasks from stalling. Younger

members may recall how Aries "got things done" and perhaps how they learned to do so with increasing empathy over time.

### Inspiring Younger Generations
If Aries becomes a coach, teacher, or informal mentor, they can pass on that "go for it" attitude. Young people might admire the way Aries overcame challenges or boldly seized chances. Hearing these stories can encourage them to be brave themselves. Aries can find deep satisfaction in seeing others adopt a confident, active mindset.

### Building Lifelong Friendships
Aries sometimes cycles through many friendships, but a few loyal connections often stand the test of time. Those who stick with Aries likely appreciate the honesty and enthusiasm, learning to handle the sign's occasional impatience. Over decades, Aries can form bonds that feel like extended family—people who share memories of adventures, efforts, and triumphs.

### Spreading Light
While Aries is not perfect, the sign's willingness to step forward can motivate entire communities. In times of crisis, an Aries might spark quick action. In times of calm, they might propose fun events. That ability to spark movement or excitement can become a kind of legacy, reminding everyone that sometimes all it takes is one person shouting, "Let's do this!" to bring people together.

## 13. Navigating Disappointments Over the Years

### High Expectations
Aries often sets the bar high—thinking they can accomplish big feats, sometimes on a short timeline. When reality does not match these hopes, disappointment can emerge. At each life stage, Aries might face challenges that do not yield quick successes: difficult college courses, delayed promotions, family disagreements, or personal health issues.

**Adapting Goals**

One of the greatest lessons for Aries is adjusting goals without losing hope. For instance, if an Aries adult wanted to open a business but finances do not line up right away, they can refine the plan, save more money, or start smaller. If a mid-life Aries feels stuck in a job, they can pivot to find new meaning rather than discarding everything abruptly. Flexibility keeps Aries from getting trapped by frustration.

**Trusting Others' Support**

Young Aries might think, "I can do it all alone." With time, they realize that sharing burdens can lighten the load. Leaning on friends, family, or colleagues for advice or help does not weaken Aries' independence—it often strengthens results. Over the decades, Aries may build a trusted network of allies.

**Healing Emotional Wounds**

At times, Aries might burn bridges or end relationships in a fit of anger or impatience. Looking back, they might regret such moments. Healing can involve reaching out, apologizing, or accepting an apology from others. An older Aries who has learned this skill can model forgiveness and understanding for younger folks.

## 14. Aries at Milestone Ages

- **At 10**: A lively child, possibly leading playground games, needing gentle reminders about waiting turns.
- **At 18**: A teen ready to test the adult world, possibly enthusiastic about the future, maybe impatient with rules.
- **At 25**: Eager to stand out in a chosen field or pivot among interests, forging new social ties, learning from quick ups and downs.

- **At 35**: Potentially established in career or family, honing a leadership style, balancing personal ambition with deeper empathy.
- **At 50**: Using wisdom from past experiences, possibly guiding younger folks, still seeking fresh challenges but with more measured steps.
- **At 65 and Beyond**: Cherishing meaningful activities, taking time to nurture family and community, still holding onto that bold spark in suitable ways.

These are broad sketches, of course. Each Aries is unique, shaped by personal background, culture, and choices. But these examples give a sense of how the Aries spirit can look at various points in life.

## 15. Continuity in the Aries Flame

Despite changes in outward behavior, Aries usually keeps a consistent core: that innate readiness to act, that hunger for direct outcomes, and that courage to say "yes" to a challenge. What shifts is how they channel these traits. Early on, it might be raw and impulsive. Later, it can be refined and strategic. But the flame rarely goes out.

**Encouraging Growth**
 Family, friends, and mentors who recognize Aries' potential can help them focus their energy. Whether it is enrolling an Aries child in sports, guiding a teen to manage strong emotions, or supporting an adult Aries in career moves, each nudge can shape the sign's growth.

**Self-Reflection**
 Aries can also assist themselves by reflecting. They might think: "How have I changed since childhood?" or "What do I still love about being bold?" By seeing how far they have come and what remains constant, Aries can understand themselves better and make positive choices at each new stage.

## 16. Challenges That Might Persist

- **Impatience**: Even seniors might show haste if forced to wait. They likely have learned coping tricks, but it can still pop up.
- **Quick Temper**: Over decades, Aries might tame it, yet certain triggers can still spark a flash of anger.
- **Boredom with Routine**: Whether a teen or a retiree, Aries might get antsy with repetitive tasks or slow environments.
- **Need for Acknowledgment**: Many Aries like to feel seen. They appreciate when others notice their actions or achievements, which can lead to seeking external validation if not balanced.

These patterns do not vanish fully but become more manageable if Aries stays self-aware. Each challenge can also be linked to a positive side—like using impatience to spark positive change or using boredom to try something new.

## 17. Positive Pathways at Each Age

### Family Foundations
In childhood and teen years, supportive adults can guide Aries to direct energy into healthy outlets, from sports to creative clubs. They can teach Aries about teamwork, showing that everyone's strengths matter.

### Peer and Career Mentors
In the twenties and thirties, Aries might find a mentor who helps shape raw ambition into a real plan. This might be a boss who recognizes Aries' drive but also teaches strategy, or a colleague who shares practical hacks for balancing tasks.

### Building Middle-Life Balance
In the forties and fifties, Aries often hits a stride: they know their strengths, their weaknesses, and what truly inspires them. They can lead teams at work, care for family, and still find a personal project

that excites them. This stage can be deeply fulfilling if Aries keeps an open mind and remains flexible.

**Wisdom and Sharing Later On**
By the sixties and beyond, Aries can become an example of a life lived with action. They can pass on stories of leaps that worked and leaps that failed, always highlighting lessons. This can encourage younger folks to be brave but mindful. Aries can also explore gentler hobbies that still offer a sense of newness—like photography, gardening (with small tasks, if we avoid the restricted term for "cultivate"), or local volunteer roles.

## 18. Adjusting to Changing Physical and Social Needs

As Aries ages, physical changes may limit certain high-impact sports. But Aries can shift to lower-impact exercises, turning them into personal challenges. Social circles may also change, with some friends moving away or focusing on different lifestyles. Aries can adapt by making new friends in new settings, keeping that dynamic nature alive.

**Staying Purposeful**
If Aries retires from a long career, they might feel restless without daily tasks. They can fill that gap by picking up part-time consulting, organizing community events, or exploring artistic projects. The sign's energy often demands an outlet, and without it, Aries might feel down.

## 19. Personal Reflection at Key Life Milestones

**Turning Points**
Birthdays that end in zero often prompt reflection. Aries might think, "Where am I now? What do I want next?" Using these turning points is helpful for Aries, as they appreciate clear markers. They can decide on fresh aims or adjust old ones.

**Recognition of Growth**

Aries, who used to dash ahead without pausing, can occasionally look back to see the personal growth. Maybe they handle stress better than at 20, or they collaborate more easily than at 30. This recognition fosters self-esteem and gratitude.

**Continuing the Fire**

No matter the age, Aries can keep that sense of lively purpose by staying curious. If a 70-year-old Aries suddenly decides to learn digital photography, it is typical Aries: direct, eager, unafraid to try something new, even if peers find it unusual. This willingness to adapt keeps them mentally and emotionally fresh.

# CHAPTER 20: SUMMING IT ALL UP

After exploring Aries from many angles—basic facts, myths, traits, family ties, love, history, confidence, daily life, personal goals, challenges, finances, public image, and more—it is time to bring it all together. Aries is known as the first sign of the zodiac, often seen as a spark that ignites new beginnings. Those born under Aries (around March 21 to April 19) are often described as bold, active, and direct. Yet, beneath that fiery reputation, there is a wide range of possible expressions. No two Aries individuals are identical, as personality also depends on family background, culture, and personal choices. However, the broad themes of Aries—bravery, initiative, strong will—tend to appear.

This final chapter will unify the main points covered, highlighting how Aries' signature energy can be harnessed for personal success and healthy relationships. We will review the sign's strengths, weaknesses, lessons learned, and the overall journey of growth. By understanding these elements, an Aries—or anyone interested in the Aries sign—can navigate life with confidence and clarity, maximizing the benefits of that Aries spark and smoothing out potential pitfalls.

## 1. Aries' Core Identity

### Fire Sign with Bold Energy
Aries, ruled traditionally by the planet Mars, carries a hot and immediate vibe. This often shows up in a readiness to move, speak, or decide. Aries likes to do something rather than wait around. This quickness can make them great problem-solvers, but it can also lead to impulsive errors if they do not pause to check all angles.

**Direct Communication**
Honesty is a hallmark. Aries typically says what they think, which can be refreshing. People know where they stand with Aries—there is rarely hidden meaning. Yet, because Aries might speak bluntly, they can unintentionally upset those who prefer gentler words. Over time, Aries can learn to keep the clarity but soften the tone.

**Natural Leadership**
Many Aries shine in leader roles, whether it is a small project team, a local club, or a big organization. Their bold spirit can rally others to action. If Aries leads with respect and listens to group members, they can form strong teams. If they ignore others' input, friction might arise. Successful Aries leaders balance self-assurance with openness.

## 2. Strengths That Stand Out

1. **Courage and Drive**: Aries seldom fears taking the first step. They press forward, even if the path is uncertain. This can create fresh opportunities that more cautious individuals might overlook.
2. **Optimism**: Aries usually believes in their ability to handle challenges. This positive outlook can encourage friends and colleagues to try new things too.
3. **High Energy**: An Aries can tackle many tasks, provided they do not burn out. Their stamina is often admired, especially when others are hesitant or tired.
4. **Protective Instinct**: Aries might defend loved ones with vigor if they sense unfair treatment. They show loyalty and stand up for those who cannot stand up for themselves.

These traits can fuel success in many fields—sports, business, the arts, activism, or leadership. Aries rarely lacks momentum. The key is using that momentum wisely.

## 3. Challenges to Manage

1. **Impatience**: Waiting can irritate Aries. They might lash out or push too hard if results are not immediate. Learning calm coping methods (like short breaks or mindful breathing) can lessen frustration.
2. **Short Temper**: Aries can flare up quickly in anger or annoyance. Over time, they can learn to spot triggers and respond more steadily, preserving harmony in relationships.
3. **Inconsistency**: Starting strong but losing interest is common if projects stretch on. Breaking tasks into mini-goals helps keep the spark alive.
4. **Overconfidence**: Aries might ignore details or advice because they trust their instincts too strongly. Accepting input from others can refine plans and prevent pitfalls.

These difficulties are not insurmountable. By being aware of them, Aries can adopt practical strategies that keep their sign's energy positive rather than destructive.

## 4. Love and Friendship

**Open-Hearted Expression**
In close bonds, Aries typically wears feelings openly. They might flirt boldly or state affection without waiting. This can be exciting for some partners, though those who prefer a slow approach may feel overwhelmed. Aries should remember to check if the other person's pace matches theirs.

**Defending Loved Ones**
Aries might jump to protect a partner, friend, or family member if they sense harm or injustice. This is a plus but can lead to confrontations if Aries does not gather facts first. Direct confrontation can fix problems fast or escalate them if not handled thoughtfully.

### Room for Independence
Aries needs a sense of personal freedom. Too many rules or constraints can build resentment. A stable relationship with Aries often allows each side some space to pursue goals individually, while also coming together for shared plans.

### Conflict Resolution
When disagreements arise, Aries might speak strongly. A calm partner or friend can help by suggesting a short pause before solutions are discussed. Over time, Aries can learn that not every conflict requires immediate, intense debate; some benefit from gentle talk.

## 5. Work, Ambitions, and Daily Life

### Action-Focused Careers
Aries does well in jobs that allow them to see the fruits of their efforts quickly—sales, event management, performing arts, sports, or any role with a fast feedback cycle. They also appreciate roles where they can lead. However, they must guard against burnout. If they pile too many tasks on themselves, stress can mount.

### Everyday Routines
At home, Aries might keep busy with projects or hobbies, but they often benefit from a loose structure to ensure chores are completed. A simple daily or weekly plan prevents Aries from neglecting dull tasks, like laundry or bills, in favor of constant excitement.

### Money Matters
Aries can handle money well if they set a short, clear system. Immediate gratification is tempting, so waiting before big purchases helps avoid regrets. Aries might enjoy earning in ways that reward effort directly, and they can learn to invest or save by treating these acts as mini-challenges with set targets.

### Public Image
Aries' directness often shapes how they are viewed. People might admire their outspokenness, though some might see them as brash. Aries can refine public impressions by sharing credit, listening politely, and handling disagreements calmly. Then, others see the boldness as a positive trait, not a threat.

## 6. Handling Emotions and Confidence

### Honest Feelings
Aries typically shows excitement, anger, sadness, or joy in a plain way. This honesty can be a relief to those who dislike guesswork. Yet Aries must remain aware of the social context—sometimes a gentler expression helps avoid hurting others.

### Confidence vs. Arrogance
Aries brims with self-belief, which can lift group morale. But if they dismiss input or seem too full of themselves, tension arises. By mixing confidence with a willingness to hear others, Aries can be an inspiring force rather than an intimidating one.

### Overcoming Fears
Although Aries appears fearless, they can have hidden doubts—like fear of failure or fear of not being recognized. A healthy approach is to face fears head-on, possibly seeking a mentor or friend's support. Admitting uncertainty can feel strange for Aries at first, but it often leads to real growth.

## 7. Growing Up and Growing Older

### Childhood
We saw that Aries children show curiosity and boldness early, often needing firm but kind boundaries. They love learning new things quickly, especially if praised for effort. Encouraging them to share toys and space with others plants the seeds of empathy.

### Teen Years

Aries adolescents want freedom and might butt heads with authority. Clear explanations of rules help them see reason. Peer influences can be strong, but Aries' self-will might protect them from following a crowd blindly. They can excel in sports or clubs that allow leadership.

### Adulthood

Young adults with Aries energy aim for achievements fast, possibly switching paths until they find a solid match. Middle-age Aries might step into leadership at work or in the community, learning to moderate their pace for the good of the team. Seniors with Aries traits keep a spirited approach, trying new pursuits or guiding younger generations with direct advice.

## 8. Spiritual or Philosophical Side

While not all Aries delve into deep spiritual beliefs, those who do might engage with them actively. They could jump into volunteer missions, group meditations (in short bursts), or personal reflection routines. Aries does not always like long, slow practices, so they might adapt spiritual pursuits to be more interactive—like mindful walks or short daily reflections. If they belong to a church or group, they may take on a leadership role or start community activities, channeling that fiery energy into shared goals.

## 9. Health and Well-Being

### Physical Outlet

Since Aries holds so much drive, physical exercise is key. Whether it is competitive sports, hiking, or short, intense workouts, these activities let Aries release stress and maintain health. It also channels restless energy.

### Preventing Burnout

Aries may try to do everything at once, risking exhaustion. Learning to take rest seriously—through short breaks or a weekly day off—helps them recharge. Over time, Aries might also incorporate calming methods, such as gentle stretching or quiet hobbies, to balance out the high tempo.

### Listening to Warnings

Ignoring minor pains or dismissing routine check-ups can backfire. Aries should remember that looking after the body is not a slowdown but a way to ensure they can keep going strong.

## 10. Aries and the World Around Them

### Group Dynamics

Aries can spark ideas in teams, clubs, or neighborhoods. They notice problems and want to fix them right away, often rallying others. If they take a breath to hear feedback, the result can be more inclusive.

### Cultural Variation

In some cultures, direct speech is welcomed, so Aries fits well. In others, it might be seen as harsh. Aries can adapt by observing local customs and adjusting their presentation, remaining true to themselves but mindful of norms.

### Innovation and Change

Aries is rarely satisfied with "We've always done it this way." They push for improvement or novelty. This can bring progress to workplaces and communities, though it might ruffle feathers among traditionalists.

## 11. Key Lessons for Aries

1. **Pause Without Losing Spark**: Before acting on impulse, taking even a brief moment to evaluate can lead to better outcomes. A short pause does not kill enthusiasm; it hones it.
2. **Listening and Collaboration**: By involving others in decisions and hearing different viewpoints, Aries multiplies their impact rather than going it alone.
3. **Manage Emotional Surges**: Recognizing triggers for anger or impatience helps Aries respond wisely. Simple techniques—like counting silently or stepping away—bring calmer results.
4. **Celebrate Others**: Aries can strengthen relationships by actively praising friends or team members. Sharing the spotlight does not dim Aries' own glow.
5. **Plan with Real Steps**: Aries can enjoy finishing tasks if they break them down. Each completed step is a satisfying checkpoint that maintains momentum.

## 12. For Those Close to an Aries

### Respect Their Drive

Aries might get frustrated if they feel held back. It helps to support them in taking action, provided that the steps are not reckless. Gentle reminders or a bit of structure can keep them on track without smothering them.

### Communicate Openly

If Aries upsets you, speak directly and calmly about it. Aries usually responds better to frank discussions than to hints. They appreciate knowing the problem instead of guessing.

### Offer Encouragement

Aries can feel lonely if no one notices their efforts. Kind words like, "I see how hard you're working," or "Your idea gave the group a big push," resonate strongly with Aries. Positive feedback can motivate them to keep going.

## 13. Aries' Future Outlook

As Aries moves through modern life, they remain a sign of possibility. Rapid shifts in technology, social norms, and work methods might actually suit Aries well, because they adapt quickly and enjoy new approaches. The sign's willingness to try fresh tactics can lead to success if guided by solid planning. For Aries individuals who manage their impulsive side, the future is wide open. They can become leaders of innovation, whether launching small startups, championing community projects, or forging brand-new ways to share knowledge.

## 14. Reflecting on Aries' Role in the Zodiac

Being the first sign, Aries is sometimes called the "baby" of the zodiac. This does not mean childishness but rather a sense of pure, direct enthusiasm—like a newborn that sees each experience as fresh and possible. Aries sets the tone for the cycle that follows in the zodiac. People often look to Aries for that first spark that says, "Things can happen now." When Aries steps forward, others might follow with their own gifts. In this sense, Aries is not just about self, but also about jumpstarting collective action. This is a powerful role, but it also brings responsibility to learn patience and listening so that everyone can move forward together.

## 15. Methods to Keep Growing

**Personal Reflection**: Even though Aries may not love long reflection, short daily notes can track achievements and struggles, revealing patterns and helping them evolve.

**Mentorships**: Finding a mentor who balances Aries' speed with wisdom can accelerate progress. Alternatively, Aries can become a mentor to younger folks, teaching them to be bold yet considerate.

**Community Involvement**: Aries thrives where immediate results show up. Volunteering for short tasks in local groups or clubs can bring a sense of purpose and tangible outcomes.

**Balanced Downtime**: Scheduling short relaxing breaks or gentle creative tasks (like painting small items or writing short stories) can keep Aries from feeling caged while still giving the mind a rest.

## 16. Embracing the Best of Aries

It might help to summarize the best qualities Aries can offer the world:

- **Fearless Beginnings**: Aries is often the one to say, "Let's start!"
- **Direct Problem-Solving**: They cut through confusion to find straightforward answers.
- **Uplifting Energy**: Aries can encourage others to act, whether in a project, a personal goal, or a fun outing.
- **Bravery in Defense**: They stand up when they see unfairness or wrongdoing, speaking out or stepping in quickly.
- **Sense of Fun**: Aries' playful side can lighten moods and create memorable times with friends or family.

## 17. Handling Weak Points with Grace

Aries' main pitfalls revolve around impatience, anger, and pushing too hard. By using the methods we have discussed—pausing before acting, listening to feedback, practicing empathy, and managing stress—Aries can reduce negative outcomes. This does not mean losing the bold spirit, but channeling it so that friction is minimized and outcomes improve.

## 18. A Continual Path

No Aries is a finished product at any age. Each new chapter of life (childhood, teen years, young adulthood, mid-life, senior years) teaches Aries something unique. Over time, they gather experiences that refine how they use their directness, courage, and passion. This pattern is ongoing, as Aries rarely sits still for too long. With each step, they can find fresh ways to be helpful, creative, and true to themselves.

## 19. Encouragement for All Aries

If you are an Aries reading this, remember that your energy is a gift. Not everyone has the ability to jump in and try something new with such vigor. When you mix that vigor with reflection, open communication, and kindness, you can reach levels of success and fulfillment that deeply satisfy you. Others might look up to you more than you realize, finding inspiration in your willingness to act. Keep refining your emotional skills, so you do not let impatience or anger overshadow your bright spirit.

If you have faced setbacks, do not give up. Aries can bounce back. Use each stumbling block as a learning experience, adjusting your approach next time. Reach out to friends or mentors if you feel stuck. Often, a short talk or bit of guidance can relight your spark. Know that your direct approach can cut through obstacles, but pacing yourself ensures you also avoid needless conflicts.

## 20. Final Wrap-Up

We have seen that Aries, while often labeled as quick and fiery, holds far more complexity than a simple stereotype. From myths and legends that highlight heroism, to modern tales of Aries individuals leading in many fields, the sign's themes shine through: courage, eagerness, a call to action, and the pursuit of fresh starts. Each Aries may express these traits in unique ways, shaped by upbringing, culture, and personal wisdom gained over time.

Stepping into an Aries viewpoint involves seeing life as an adventure that needs someone to spark it. Aries might be the one who says "Let's go!" and pulls everyone out of hesitation. Yet the greatest Aries figures also learn that leading does not mean ignoring others, and acting quickly does not require skipping all caution. Blending speed with thought, boldness with empathy, and strength with humility leads to a well-rounded Aries presence that can transform families, workplaces, and communities.

Wherever you or the Aries person in your life stands—child, teen, adult, or elder—there is always potential to refine that signature flame. By understanding Aries traits, harnessing them well, and building on the practical tips provided, one can shape a life marked by achievements, strong bonds, and a genuine sense of purpose. Aries is a sign of sparks and action, and when guided by insight, that spark not only lights up the Aries individual but also warms and excites the people around them.

This concludes our look at Aries. May it empower all who resonate with Aries energy—or who care about an Aries—to appreciate the gifts of directness, drive, and courage, while also handling the challenges. The Aries spark has led to countless breakthroughs throughout history, and it can continue to do so in everyday life. With mindful growth, each Aries can stay true to their dynamic core, lighting the way forward and inspiring everyone who sees that bright flame in action.

# Help Us Share Your Thoughts!

**Dear reader,**

Thank you for spending your time with this book. We hope it brought you enjoyment and a few new ideas to think about. If there was anything that didn't work for you, or if you have suggestions on how we can improve, please let us know at **kontakt@skriuwer.com**. Your feedback means a lot to us and helps us make our books even better.

If you enjoyed this book, we would be very grateful if you left a review on the site where you purchased it. Your review not only helps other readers find our books, but also encourages us to keep creating more stories and materials that you'll love.

By choosing Skriuwer, you're also supporting **Frisian**—a minority language mainly spoken in the northern Netherlands. Although **Frisian** has a rich history, the number of speakers is shrinking, and it's at risk of dying out. Your purchase helps fund resources to preserve and promote this language, such as educational programs and learning tools. If you'd like to learn more about Frisian or even start learning it yourself, please visit **www.learnfrisian.com**.

Thank you for being part of our community. We look forward to sharing more books with you in the future.

**Warm regards,**
The Skriuwer Team

www.ingramcontent.com/pod-product-compliance
Lightning Source LLC
LaVergne TN
LVHW012039070526
838202LV00056B/5541